Psychopathy: A Very Short Introduction

VERY SHORT INTRODUCTIONS are for anyone wanting a stimulating and accessible way into a new subject. They are written by experts, and have been translated into more than 45 different languages.

The series began in 1995, and now covers a wide variety of topics in every discipline. The VSI library currently contains over 600 volumes—a Very Short Introduction to everything from Psychology and Philosophy of Science to American History and Relativity—and continues to grow in every subject area.

Very Short Introductions available now:

Available soon:

For more information visit our website

www.oup.com/vsi/

Essi Viding

PSYCHOPATHY

A Very Short Introduction

OXFORD
UNIVERSITY PRESS

OXFORD

UNIVERSITY PRESS

Great Clarendon Street, Oxford, OX2 6DP,
United Kingdom

Oxford University Press is a department of the University of Oxford.
It furthers the University's objective of excellence in research, scholarship,
and education by publishing worldwide. Oxford is a registered trade mark of
Oxford University Press in the UK and in certain other countries

Published in the United States of America by Oxford University Press
198 Madison Avenue, New York, NY 10016, United States of America

British Library Cataloguing in Publication Data
Data available

Library of Congress Control Number: 2019941478

ISBN 978-0-19-880226-6

Printed in Great Britain by
Ashford Colour Press Ltd., Gosport, Hampshire.

For Ava and Milo

Contents

Preface

During my undergraduate degree in psychology at University College London (UCL) I was particularly drawn to courses that explored the workings of the brain or focused on different disorders. Like the rest of the world, it seems, I was fascinated by what makes some people 'evil' and psychopathic. It was puzzling to me that a person could be capable of premeditated extreme violence or would not feel sorry for a fellow human being who was frightened or hurt.

I was lucky to take a final year course where much of the teaching was given by Dr James Blair, one of the world's foremost experts in psychopathy. I started the course with several misconceptions of what psychopathy is and what psychopaths do. My vision was coloured by the film *The Silence of the Lambs*, and I pictured clever, suave, manipulative serial killers with a chilling block of ice where their heart should have been. The course introduced me to the state of the art in psychopathy research and helped me develop a more nuanced understanding of the condition than that which was afforded by watching Hollywood films.

James was able to vividly convey how individuals with psychopathy lacked a normal response to other people's distress. While most of us refrain from hurting others—emotionally or physically—because imagining or seeing others in distress is deeply uncomfortable for us, research by James had shown that other people's distress simply does not have the same kind of impact on psychopaths or those at risk of developing the disorder. The course also introduced me to the work of Robert Hare, Joe Newman, Chris Patrick, Scott Lilienfeld, and others, who had demonstrated that in addition to their inability to resonate with other people's distress, psychopaths seemed unable to learn from bad experiences, could appear fearless, and were able to manipulate people without any qualms.

I did all the course reading, and more. I applied for and got a research assistant position in James Blair's group after my first degree and spent the following two years collecting data in prisons and in schools for children with behavioural difficulties. I then went on to complete PhD and post-doctoral research with Professor Francesca Happé and Professor Robert Plomin at King's College London. Under their supervision I learned more about ways to investigate how children with psychopathic traits think and what might cause their personality features and behaviour.

I now lead a research group at UCL that dedicates a substantial amount of its effort to studying why psychopathy develops. In this book I provide a readable account of psychopathy research that helps illuminate the condition and how it develops. This is not intended to be a comprehensive overview of the field, which would be beyond the scope of a *Very Short Introduction*. I am also doubtful that everything that scientists in the field focus on would be of equal interest to the public.

Before I started writing this book, I discussed the content with some close friends and academic colleagues who are not psychopathy researchers. I asked them what they would find interesting and helpful to know, and what I cover in this book is in part informed by those discussions. Another psychopathy researcher may have chosen to write the book differently and there are some very good popular science books on psychopathy out there. I have listed a few as further reading and strongly recommend that an interested reader take a look at them. I also hope that the readers of this *Very Short Introduction* find it informative. It is unique in its strong focus on the experimental studies of the psychopathic mind and its consideration of the development of psychopathy. I have greatly enjoyed writing about these areas of research and surveying not only what we know, but also what we still need to find out about this fascinating condition.

Acknowledgements

Uta Frith first encouraged me to think about writing this book. She was not interested in hearing about 'the million reasons why I should not go ahead with it', offered up by the fairly loud impostor syndrome voice inside my head. Both Uta and Eamon McCrory, who co-directs the research unit at UCL with me, offered invaluable advice regarding the structure of the book. Without Eamon, I would not have done some of my most exciting research into the development of psychopathy; ours is a truly collaborative effort.

A British Academy Mid-Career Fellowship enabled me to have a teaching sabbatical, which provided time to write. David Thurston, Barbara Maughan, and Olivia Bishop all lent their beautiful homes for child-free writing retreats, and without their generosity there would be no book. Inti Brazil and anonymous reviewers gave insightful feedback that helped improve the book. Philip Kelly, Leonardo Bevilacqua, César Lima, John Rogers, and Ana Seara-Cardoso created some of the illustrations. Harriet Phillips helped with the indexing. Jenny Nugee and Andrea Keegan gave fantastic editorial input.

I have been incredibly lucky to have brilliant collaborators, mentors, students, colleagues and friends with whom I have exchanged ideas over the years and who have constantly challenged my thinking about psychopathy. It is not possible to name everyone without making this book *A Not So Very Short Introduction*, but I want to particularly thank Robert Plomin, Francesca Happé, Geoff Bird, Charlotte Cecil, Sara Clarke, Stephane de Brito, Nathalie Fontaine, Lucy Foulkes, Annie Gaule, Alice Jones, Henrik Larsson, Patricia Lockwood, Liz O'Nions, Jean-Baptiste Pingault, Ruth Roberts, Ana Seara-Cardoso, Catherine Sebastian, Arjun Sethi, James Blair, Paul Frick, Terrie Moffitt, John Morton, Arielle Baskin-Sommers, Craig Neumann, Kent Kiehl, Abigail Marsh, Don Lynam, Sam Mornington, Louise Arseneault, Alice Gregory, Nikolaus Steinbeis, Fred Dick, Eloise Millar, and Liz Lee. Many more feature in the pages of this book.

My family in Finland, Mum and Dad, Anna and Jussi (and their delightful 'add-ons') all tolerated holiday disappearances to write. John enabled child-free writing retreats and other disappearances to write. Most importantly, John, Ava, and Milo made sure that I had a life when writing this book, while displaying a reassuring degree of empathy at critical junctures.

List of illustrations

Introduction

Psychopathy has long captured the public imagination. Newspaper column inches have been devoted to murderers with psychopathic features. As is evident by the success of films such as *We Need to Talk About Kevin* and *No Country for Old Men* (Figures 1a and 1b), Hollywood and audiences worldwide have also been fascinated and repulsed in equal measure by characters who are exceptionally cold and callous. We now understand psychopathy as a personality disorder characterized by lack of empathy and guilt, manipulation of other people, a tendency to make bafflingly destructive life choices, and, in the case of criminal psychopathy, capacity for premeditated violent behaviour. Financially, psychopaths generate substantial societal costs in relation to their incarceration and failure to consistently contribute to the workforce. Perhaps more importantly, they can inflict immeasurable emotional, psychological, and financial costs on their victims.

Despite public fascination with psychopathy, there is often a very limited understanding of the condition, and several myths about psychopathy abound. For example, people commonly assume that psychopaths are sadistic serial killers or that all violent and antisocial individuals are psychopaths. Yet, systematic research over the past 35–40 years convincingly shows that most psychopaths are not responsible for multiple homicides. Equally,

1. The films *We Need to Talk About Kevin* (a) and *No Country for Old Men* (b) both featured callous psychopaths who went on to murder people in cold blood.

there are plenty of antisocial and violent offenders who are not psychopaths. It is not antisocial behaviour and violence in themselves that characterize psychopathy; it is the profound absence of empathy and guilt that is at the core of what makes a psychopath, and what sets such individuals apart from the rest of us.

The research into psychopathy is proceeding at a healthy pace and we know so much more than we did even ten years ago. But much also remains a mystery and a focus of continued research efforts. Is psychopathy a genetic condition? Do people become psychopaths because of their childhood experiences? As children, were there signs that could have warned us that someone is at risk of developing psychopathy? Can psychopathy be prevented or treated? Are all psychopaths criminals? These questions and many others occupy researchers (including myself), policymakers, clinicians, educators, and also the public.

The reasons for pursuing these questions are manifold. I think it is very human to be fascinated by a condition that renders someone so 'alien', lacking in basic human qualities of empathy, concern, guilt, and care for other people. Many of us want to understand how individuals with psychopathy see the world, what 'makes them tick', how and why they end up behaving the way they do. Perhaps part of this interest relates to our fear of psychopaths and the need to understand how they operate so that we might avoid the danger they pose. There is also no doubt that individuals with psychopathy are costly to society (some estimates put the cost at ten times that which is associated with depression) and this makes them top of policymakers' worry lists as individuals that we need to do something about. As a psychologist interested in development, I am personally keen to understand why children develop this way. No one is born a psychopath. Could systematic research give us tools to help individuals at risk and their families? Questions like these form the backbone of what I want to consider in this book.

3

Chapter 1

How can we know if someone is a psychopath or is at risk of becoming one?

If the public perception of psychopaths as bloodthirsty serial killers is not universally accurate, then what are individuals with psychopathy like, what are their defining features? And how can we know if someone is a psychopath or at risk of developing the disorder? Before delving into the science, let's consider some case studies. These cases are closely based on individuals that I have encountered via my research, as well as those documented by colleagues in the field. They give a flavour of the developmental course of criminal psychopathy, as well as what a person without criminal convictions, but a host of psychopathic personality traits, looks like.

Mark

Mark was the second-born child of Lisa and Tom. Following the unplanned birth of their first child, Tom had to leave college and take a job at the local storage facility. As a result, the family struggled financially. Lisa recalls that Mark was a difficult baby, often 'screaming in rage' and rarely returning affection for his parents. He did not respond to Lisa's attempts to engage with him, often looking away when Lisa was talking to him. Lisa says that Mark always struck her as very different from his older sister. As a toddler, he was frequently violent towards other children, trying to hurt them when he thought grown-ups were not looking. He was also cruel to the family pet and could not be left alone with it. He would deliberately break his big sister's toys and there were many instances when he hit, kicked, and bit her very hard. He appeared fearless and immune to any punishment, such as being made to sit on the 'naughty step' to have a time out. He showed little empathy for others and when he was asked to imagine how his behaviour might make other people feel, he simply looked blank.

At school Mark's problems escalated and he was eventually transferred to a special school for children with behavioural difficulties. This was in sharp contrast to his sister, who did well at school and had many friends. By adolescence, Mark's behaviour at school was characterized by aggression, bullying, blackmail of other boys, attempts to intimidate members of staff, and lack of regret for his actions. No sanctions imposed by the school staff seemed to have any effect on Mark. Eventually, Mark started to skip school and by his mid-teens got involved in a number of burglaries and robberies. His parents were not able to monitor his activities, and Mark began to routinely hang out with delinquent peers, but did not seem to have firm friends. Acquaintances seemed to come and go depending on whether they were of use to him. He would often implicate his peers if he was caught doing something, in order to save his own skin.

Eventually, in his late teens, he received a prison sentence for a violent robbery. When he was released from prison he continued his criminal lifestyle. He never settled down with a family but had a string of girlfriends, two of whom became pregnant. Mark showed little interest in his children and failed to provide any financial support for them. He was engaged in supplying drugs, was involved in several financial scams, and ended up jailed for a second time for killing his criminal partner following a disagreement about money. As an adult, Mark's prison file was reviewed and he was interviewed by the prison psychologist. The psychologist noted that Mark rarely expressed any guilt or remorse for killing his friend, seemed incapable of feeling empathy, was happy to manipulate other people, did not fulfil his obligations to his children, and engaged in a wide variety of criminal behaviours. Although Mark's psychopathic traits have manifested in different ways at different ages, at each point in his development his behaviours were striking by the degree to which they differed from the behaviour of his peers and demonstrated a profound lack of empathy or concern for the rights and welfare of others.

David

David was the first-born child of Susan and Michael. His family was solidly educated and middle-class, his father was a solicitor, and his mother worked part-time as a teacher. The birth was uneventful and, although David was not the calmest baby, Susan did not recall anything out of the ordinary. As a toddler David could be aggressive and was extremely possessive of his toys, but again Susan was not unduly worried at this point. However, Susan recalls that as David went to nursery and school, she would find herself often feeling uneasy because of his sense of entitlement and seeming lack of concern for friends' or family members' needs and well-being. She says that David would be able to turn on the charm when he wanted something, but would get angry and unpleasant if he did not get what he wanted. Both parents recall that compared to his younger brother, David seemed to care very little about pleasing his parents and would not feel bad if he had made his mother or father sad. Michael recalls that he thought that David would often lie and would not take responsibility for his actions, but David would vehemently insist on his version of the events even if it was blatantly wrong. David did not seem to have typical friendships. He did not show loyalty to people and he hung out with boys who did his bidding.

David was relatively lazy at school, but with the help of some tutoring he finished school with reasonable grades and was admitted to a good university where he studied economics. In his second year at university the faculty suspected him of coercing another student to write his coursework essays, but this could not be proven. Since late adolescence, David dated multiple girlfriends, sometimes several at one go, and he never stayed in one relationship for very long. He was unreliable with arrangements and while he could be very charming to begin with, he would soon turn mean and controlling and would blame the girlfriend for any relationship failures and disappointments. David would often borrow money from his girlfriends and parents, but almost always failed to pay them back. His parents also reported that they thought David was at times stealing from them.

After university, David gained a place on a training scheme of a well-known financial institution. He had presented very confidently at the interview and was domineering and ruthless during his training. He was happy to take credit for work he had not done, would spread false rumours of his colleagues and their competence, always blamed other members of the team for any mistakes, and blackmailed his immediate line manager into writing him a glowing reference after discovering some sensitive personal information about her. After departing his first job for a new position in another firm, it also transpired that there was false information in David's CV. However, this revelation went unchallenged as the previous line manager was too scared to confront David.

In his new job David was put in charge of overseeing a small team of people. His team members soon confided in their close friends that they found it highly stressful to work with David and that there was low morale among the staff. They found him unpredictable and unable to lead the project, but he would always blame others for any failures. A female colleague reported being sexually coerced by David, but withdrew her accusations after receiving threatening and manipulative anonymous calls. Although David has avoided any formal criminal proceedings so far and seems to function in mainstream society, it is clear to see that, like Mark, he also demonstrates a profound lack of empathy or concern for the rights and welfare of others.

How can we know for sure that Mark and David have psychopathy? The origins of the current description of the psychopathy syndrome can be traced back to the work of Harvey Cleckley in 1940s, and his book, *The Mask of Sanity*. Some of the key features of psychopathy recorded by Cleckley included: absence of nervousness, interpersonal charm, lack of shame, impoverished affect (emotions seem shallow and are often used to manipulate others), and antisocial behaviour that appears senseless and without obvious motivation. Since Cleckley's days, scientists have systematically developed ways of assessing psychopathy in criminal populations and in community samples. They have also developed assessments for psychopathic traits in children.

How do we know if a criminal is a psychopath?

From the criteria delineated by Cleckley, and his own clinical impressions, Robert Hare developed the Psychopathy Checklist in the 1980s. The Psychopathy Checklist is a formalized tool for the assessment of psychopathy in incarcerated adults, using recorded file information and semi-structured interviews by trained professionals. Together with his colleagues, Robert Hare conducted careful studies to validate and revise the instrument, demonstrating that it effectively and reliably captures psychopathic features and predicts future behaviour.

The Psychopathy Checklist is the most widely used instrument for assessing psychopathy in criminal justice system settings. Individuals are rated on thirty items that capture lack of empathy and guilt, emotions that are short-lived and do not appear genuine, manipulation of others, grandiose sense of self-worth, failure to take care of their obligations, using others for their own gain, and versatile and prolific patterns of antisocial behaviour that start in early childhood. Someone would be rated as lacking empathy and guilt if their file information showed a track record of treating others cruelly and failure to express remorse for their offences, and if during their interview they would mainly lament the fact that they are incarcerated, rather than the pain they have caused their victims. Manipulation of others and a grandiose sense of self-worth would be rated if the file information and interviews showed evidence of deceiving other people financially, coercing other people to antisocial acts that benefit the offender, and considering themselves as more deserving and capable than other people.

File information and interviews are also used to collect evidence regarding crime, length of criminal career, and seriousness of offences. Only a subset of criminals in the justice system have the full set of characteristics that would earn them the psychopathy label using the Hare criteria. These individuals are not merely irresponsible, impulsive, or aggressive. They are also characterized by profound lack of empathy for their fellow human beings, lack of remorse, pathological lying, sense of entitlement, and ability to manipulate others for their own gain. Mark would certainly fit this description.

Antisocial, sociopath, psychopath—what is in the name?

The public narrative often uses the terms antisocial (or antisocial personality disordered), sociopath, and psychopath interchangeably. As a result, it is easy to be confused and wonder whether individuals with psychopathy are just people with extreme antisocial personality disorder or whether sociopathy and psychopathy refer to the same thing. Why do we have all these different labels—could we not just use one label to avoid confusion?

Antisocial personality disorder

Diagnostic classification systems, such as the American Psychiatric Association's Diagnostic and Statistical Manual (known as DSM-5), outline symptoms and guidance for clinical professionals who diagnose psychiatric disorders. Although the standard assessment of criminal psychopathy using the Hare criteria is as, if not more rigorous than traditional psychiatric diagnostic assessments based on classification systems such as DSM-5, psychopathy is not included as a formal diagnosis in these systems. Instead, the DSM-5 has a diagnostic category called antisocial personality disorder, which refers to individuals who violate societal norms and rights of other people.

To gain a diagnosis of antisocial personality disorder according to the DSM-5, a person has to be eighteen, their antisocial behaviour should not be explained by another disorder (such as schizophrenia), they should have a history of clinically significant behavioural problems since childhood (termed conduct disorder in diagnostic manuals), and they must display *one or more* forms of antisocial behaviour. The clinician conducting a diagnostic assessment might look for evidence of criminal arrest, consistent lying and deception, harmful impulsive decisions and behaviours, aggressive behaviour, putting others in danger, not taking care of one's obligations and responsibilities, and lack of remorse.

It should be evident to the reader that it is possible for people with very different presentations to gain the diagnosis. Two individuals—one who lies and manipulates and lacks remorse for using and deceiving others, like Mark in our case study example, and another who, unlike Mark, is capable of remorse, but is regularly irritable and has difficulty in controlling their anger and emotional outbursts—could both be diagnosed as having antisocial personality disorder if they were at least eighteen at the time of assessment and had a childhood history of problem behaviour. In other words, the antisocial personality disorder criteria capture a motley crew of individuals whose presentation and reasons for antisocial behaviour can vary considerably and include both those who would meet the Hare criteria for psychopathy and those who do not. Put differently, those individuals who are classified as psychopaths based on the Hare criteria would qualify for antisocial personality disorder diagnosis, but most individuals with an antisocial personality diagnosis do not qualify for psychopathy as they would not display the profound lack of empathy and remorse that are characteristic of the condition (Figure 2).

Because psychopaths are profoundly emotionally different from you and me, and also from the majority of other criminals who

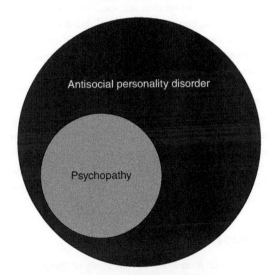

2. Antisocial personality disorder does not equate to psychopathy. Although most individuals with psychopathy would qualify for an antisocial personality disorder diagnosis, the converse is not true. Many more individuals qualify for an antisocial personality disorder diagnosis than have psychopathy.

11

qualify for antisocial personality disorder, we would want to systematically identify the condition, rather than just talk about severe antisocial personality disorder. Someone who lacks empathy and remorse is likely to need very different treatment and risk assessment considerations than someone else, whose primary problem is in regulating their impulses or emotions.

Sociopathy

Descriptions of sociopathy include accounts of antisocial and violent acts and failure to stick to societal responsibilities, as well as diminished concern for the welfare of others. Sociopaths are often described as being unfeeling towards others, selfishly pursuing their own needs and using aggression to get what they want. Despite a vague sense that sociopathy denotes serious antisocial behaviour, no separate, well-validated assessment instrument for sociopathy exists. There are self-report questionnaires that claim to assess sociopathic attitudes, but these are rarely used in research studies or criminal justice settings. In short, sociopathy is a label that chiefly exists to denote serious antisocial behaviour in public speak—but is ill-defined and not used in mainstream scientific research or clinical/justice system assessments. It would be better if this term would fade from use altogether, yet it appears curiously popular in the media and a quick Google search reveals several articles that purport to help the reader to spot whether they are in a relationship with a sociopath or if their boss may be one.

The psychopath near you

Chillingly, as can be seen with the case study of David, there are also individuals with psychopathic features who function in mainstream society and never commit outright crimes—or at least never get caught or reported. We know relatively little about these individuals, but are becoming increasingly aware of the fact that even if they stay on the right side of the law (or avoid detection), they cause a lot of heartache and havoc to those around them. Empathy and concern for others and following societal obligations are such fundamental human qualities that a lack of these qualities can have devastating social consequences.

Careful studies suggest that we can reliably measure psychopathic traits in the general population. In other words, people vary in their level of psychopathic traits, and all of us are somewhere along the continuum of being more or less psychopathic. When I talk about this with friends and students, they can usually readily identify colleagues, acquaintances, or family members (or presidents!) who behave in ways that might indicate higher than average levels of psychopathic traits.

Psychopathic traits in community samples cannot be assessed using Hare's Psychopathy Checklist, as it is designed for those in the criminal justice system. Most people do not have fat dossiers detailing their case history (i.e. the 'file information' that is critical for formal psychopathy assessments) and it is hard to imagine that people would queue up to take part in semi-structured interviews designed to probe whether they are psychopaths. (Although some may! I am reminded of a work dinner that unusually had a high concentration of both scientists and business people. Upon finding out what I do, several businessmen lined up to offer that either they themselves or their 'colleague so-and-so' was likely to be a psychopath. I was lost for words.) However, several instruments such as the Self-Report Psychopathy Scale, the Psychopathic Personality Inventory, and the Triarchic Psychopathy Measure have been developed for the assessment of psychopathic personality traits in community samples. These instruments have been scientifically validated using large samples and they reliably capture population variation in identified psychopathic qualities.

Although we can reliably measure psychopathic personality traits in community samples, we have less systematic research that tells us where people with such traits end up and how they live their lives. From time to time newspapers run articles declaiming that particular professionals, such as business leaders, lawyers, or politicians, are likely to be psychopaths. Reassuringly most people in these professions are very unlikely to have worryingly high levels of psychopathic traits, but tentative findings suggest that certain professions, such as business management, may have a higher concentration of individuals with multiple psychopathic features. Perhaps no surprise there, but we are still waiting for studies that would quantify the rates of people with high levels of psychopathic traits across different professions.

We are also not sure why some people with high levels of psychopathic traits do not end up in the criminal system. Professor Adrian Raine from the University of Pennsylvania has conducted interesting research that suggests that psychopathic individuals with higher intelligence may be better at not getting caught for their crimes, or commit acts that are antisocial and unpleasant, but for which they cannot be charged under law (he has called these individuals 'successful psychopaths'). If such individuals do get caught, they often receive ample media attention, because their conduct has been particularly brazen, destructive, and chilling. Such stories have bolstered the notion of the psychopath as a highly intelligent predator, but on average those with high levels of psychopathic traits score a little lower on assessments of cognitive ability than their peers. It is unclear what explains this finding, but researchers have speculated that antisocial behaviours commonly associated with psychopathic traits may limit educational opportunities for most individuals with high levels of psychopathic traits, and in turn lead to worse performance in some formal tests of cognitive ability. However, like the rest of us, these individuals span a wide range of cognitive ability. And, like David in our second case study, some have higher than average intellectual capacity and manage to stay on the right side of the law. Even so, most of us would not want to have them as our boss or romantic partner.

In David's (as well as Mark's) cases, manifestations of psychopathic traits and behaviours were evident from early childhood. Could something have been done to prevent the unpleasant and frightening behaviours that David and Mark engaged in as adults? Can we reliably recognize psychopathic traits in children?

Are there psychopathic children?

No one gets psychopathic personality disorder as a surprise birthday present when they turn eighteen. Yet I would not advocate labelling children as psychopaths. The label of 'psychopath' has connotations of an individual being depraved, dangerous, and beyond redemption, but like any other feature of our personality, psychopathic traits and their behavioural manifestations can change over development and can change following intervention. As such it would be overly harsh and irresponsible to use the psychopathy label in reference to children whose developmental outcomes are not fixed. I prefer to talk about developmental risk for psychopathy or psychopathic traits/ features when I discuss my research on children, and these are the terms that I will use in this book. Regardless, it is clear that the traits that characterize adults with psychopathy can also be observed in children and reliably used to predict increased risk for persistent antisocial behaviour.

The first attempt to characterize psychopathic features in children was John Bowlby's 1940s description of 'affectionless psychopathy'. It mirrored some of the key features introduced by Cleckley (such as lack of responsiveness to the suffering of others), but lay forgotten for a long time until Professor Paul Frick, a developmental psychologist working at Louisiana State University, devised the first formal measure of indexing psychopathic traits in children. A number of well-validated measures by Frick and others, varying in their length and coverage of different aspects of psychopathic personality, now exist for children. These measures have been shown to successfully identify children at risk of persistent antisocial behaviour/psychopathy.

Formal diagnostic schemes for conduct disorder (the diagnostic label for children with clinically concerning levels of antisocial behaviour) have traditionally captured many of the antisocial, impulsive, and interpersonal aspects associated with psychopathic presentation (some of which are shared with other individuals with antisocial behaviour). These include acts of aggression (e.g. violent robbery, cruelty to people and animals), destruction of property, stealing, lying, and serious violation of rules (e.g. truanting from school, running away from home).

A diagnosis of conduct disorder is given only if a child or young person has been repeatedly antisocial and this has manifested in at least three different ways in the past year. The disturbance in behaviour also has to be sufficiently serious to cause significant impairment in social relationships, for education, or at work. Much like antisocial personality disorder, conduct disorder symptom criteria also capture a varied set of individuals, who may not have any symptom overlap. Furthermore, the majority of these children do not show features that set those at risk of developing psychopathy apart from other antisocial individuals.

Finally, the diagnostic classification systems have not always consistently assessed lack of empathy and remorse, as well as shallow affect. After careful consideration of decades of research findings, the most recent revision of DSM-5 added symptoms to their conduct disorder criteria in order to capture some of the personality traits and behaviours that index risk of developing psychopathy. These include lack of remorse or guilt, callous lack of empathy, shallow or deficient affect, and lack of concern about performance. A clinician assessing these features might probe parents or teachers to consider whether the child is remorseful if they have hurt someone, whether the child is concerned about the feelings of others and cares for them, whether the child is concerned about fulfilling obligations or whether they blame others for their failures, and whether their emotions seem sincere (or are used only when essential for manipulating others).

In line with the DSM-5 approach, many researchers, myself included, have used a measure of callous-unemotional traits alongside measurement of conduct disorder symptoms to identify children at risk of developing psychopathy. In doing so we often come up against natural concerns about labelling children, and whether we are at risk of pathologizing behaviours that might be typical at certain ages. Most children and young people can act in selfish and defiant ways and that does not mean they have conduct disorder or are at risk of developing psychopathy.

Here it is important to reiterate that a child or young person would not be identified as 'at risk' unless their behaviour was extremely concerning (atypical when the child is compared with their same age peers) and causing harm to their social relationships, education, or work—as well as to those around them. In other words, someone who has engaged in occasional mischief or a few acts of teenage rebellion would not get a clinical referral or be invited to take part in our research. Those with conduct disturbance or who are at risk of developing psychopathy—as assessed by validated instruments—look very different from their peers and are at increased risk of long-term problems. The current assessment tools capture a group of children that we need to understand better, so that it is possible to help them and their families, as well as those people outside the family who are involved in these children's lives.

How common is psychopathy?

Scientists estimate that just under 1 per cent of the population would qualify for criminal psychopathy diagnosis according to the Hare's Psychopathy Checklist criteria. This may seem like a low number, but these individuals represent the most prolific, dangerous, and violent offenders and are thought to be responsible for more than half of all serious crime. Although the Hare Psychopathy Checklist successfully identifies dangerous individuals, there is no scientific evidence that those scoring above the cut-off represent a 'distinct class'. In some ways drawing a diagnostic line on a condition that represents an extreme of a number of dimensions (lack of empathy, impulsivity, etc.) is artificial. Someone who falls just short of an official diagnostic cut-off is also likely to be worrisome and will exhibit a considerably more pathological presentation than an average person in their peer group. Regardless, the cut-off does identify people who are reliably of concern and this can be helpful for risk assessment purposes.

We do not diagnose members of the general public as psychopaths (although we can say that someone scores among the top 5 per cent of the general population on psychopathic traits, for example). Similarly, a child will not receive a diagnosis of psychopathy, but we can index those at highest risk of developing the condition by selecting children with conduct disorder who also display clinically concerning levels of psychopathic traits. If we extrapolate from what we know about the prevalence of conduct disorder and the proportion of those children who also have clinically concerning levels of psychopathic traits, then we can estimate that between 1.5 and 2 per cent of children would be indexed as having developmental risk for psychopathy.

Many more men than women are diagnosed with criminal psychopathy. We do not have precise estimates for the ratio of male to female psychopaths, but if we make calculations based on what we know about rates of antisocial and criminal behaviour in males vs. females, it is perhaps safe to expect the ratio to be around five male criminal psychopaths to every one female criminal psychopath. However, this figure should be digested in the context of criminal convictions being a lot more common in males than in females. The behavioural expressions of psychopathic personality may vary in males and females, and this may in part explain the differences in rates of criminal psychopathy diagnosis.

There are cultural and physical constraints on behaviour that likely mean that the same personality features manifest in different ways in men and women. Cultural norms dictate that different behaviours are going to be more or less acceptable for men and women, and this implies that a successful strategy for getting what you want and looking after number one will not necessarily always be the same for both sexes. Similarly, physical size will constrain whether you will be able to reliably intimidate or physically aggress against other people. Research shows that women with psychopathy are much more likely to engage in relational aggression (spreading rumours, exclusion, mean comments), while men with psychopathy are much more likely to be physically aggressive. These findings are in line with the notion that differences in societal expectations and physical size may play a role in who is diagnosed with criminal psychopathy.

The importance of having a clear definition of psychopathy

I keep returning to the fact that individuals with psychopathy are a societal burden and also cause an untold amount of suffering. This is why it is important to be able to recognize and study them. We can now reliably identify individuals with psychopathic traits across different settings and developmental stages and we are beginning to better understand psychopathy in females.

We know that individuals with psychopathic traits are not merely impulsive or aggressive, but they also fail to care for the well-being of others. Careful research has also shown us that whether we look at criminal psychopaths, individuals with high levels of psychopathic traits in the general population, or children who are at risk of developing psychopathy, we see similar patterns of brain function and information processing. Some of these patterns are unique to individuals with psychopathic features and are not seen in other people with antisocial behaviour. Research also tells us that risk factors associated with psychopathic features (both genetic and environmental) may not be fully identical to those seen for antisocial behaviour more broadly. Such data give us additional confidence that the assessment measures for psychopathy are capturing something meaningful. Having found ways to identify psychopaths, researchers are able to conduct studies that systematically advance our understanding of why such individuals behave in the way they do, how this condition develops, and whether there is any hope of preventing or treating psychopathy.

Chapter 2

Explaining the lack of empathy

A marked lack of empathy is one of the hallmarks of psychopathy. Mark and David, who appear in the case studies in Chapter 1, both have a track record of behaving in ways that show a profound lack of feeling for other people or concern for their well-being. When Mark was asked to imagine how his callous behaviour made other people feel, he simply looked blank. David was happy to blackmail his colleague, although this was clearly something that caused distress. Witnessing this inability to resonate with other people is chilling and troubling.

I vividly recall conducting a research assessment on a prisoner who was serving a life sentence for murder. At the time of meeting him, I did not know whether he was a psychopath or not (we did all of our testing 'blind' to the status of the offenders), but I had my suspicions following the encounter. Part of the assessment involved giving the prisoners a task of viewing faces with different emotional expressions. We tested whether they had difficulty in recognizing the expressions. Most of the time our participants did fairly well on this task, although some (the psychopaths as it later turned out) had trouble picking up that someone was looking scared.

On the whole the testing sessions were unremarkable and I remember very few of the individual prisoners we saw for the study. However, this particular testing occasion stayed with me.

Every time a fearful face appeared on the screen, the prisoner in question seemed unable to identify the emotion. Most participants in our study got there in the end, even if it took them a little longer, but not him. Finally, he turned to me and said: 'I really do not know what that emotion is, but I do know that it is what people look like just before I stab them.'

Of course, being able to name emotions does not itself guarantee that someone is empathetic. It is also possible that without complete formal education (as is the case with many prisoners), someone may simply not have the vocabulary to correctly name all emotions, even if they can empathize with them. Two things are worth noting in this context. First, all other participants in our study, including participants with psychopathy, were able to name all of the emotional expressions we showed them (i.e. they knew the vocabulary), those with psychopathy just found it more difficult to identify fear fast and reliably. Second, the most harrowing aspect of my encounter with this prisoner was not the fact that he was not able to find the correct word. It was the fact that he recognized the expression from the context of having been violent towards other people, yet it prompted no discernible emotional reaction in him. He might just as well have been talking about buying a loaf of bread. Psychopaths do not have the same capacity for human feeling as the rest of us, they do not appear moved by the things that usually deeply affect others, such as seeing fellow human beings suffer or in distress. And this is perhaps why they do not experience genuine remorse for the hurt and misfortune that they inflict. This lack of empathy and remorse, combined with the propensity for manipulating others and the ability to present a good front when it benefits 'the number one', prompted Harvey Cleckley to exclaim that psychopaths 'know the words, but they do not know the music'.

Why do psychopaths not find it disturbing when someone is distressed, frightened, or in pain? Why are they so different from the rest of us, who find it deeply unpleasant and unsettling to witness other people's discomfort and distress? Are they similar or different to individuals on the autism spectrum who can sometimes behave in ways that appear uncaring? What are the brain bases of the empathy deficits we see in individuals with psychopathy? These questions have fascinated researchers for several decades and we now have some clues regarding how the thoughts and emotions (what we can broadly call 'cognitions') of psychopaths are atypical in ways that help explain their callous disregard for others. We also know that the brains of psychopaths are different—unsurprisingly as they behave so differently from the rest of us.

Collectively, research has found that individuals with psychopathic features process emotions differently from their peers, which is thought to explain their lack of empathy and guilt. We can see this in children at risk of developing psychopathy, as well as adults with high levels of psychopathic traits, whether they live in mainstream society or have been convicted as criminals. Both children and adults with psychopathic features also have similar atypical neural processing patterns when they perform tasks that require processing of other people's distress and pain, or one's own feelings of guilt.

In this chapter I want to give you a flavour of the kinds of tasks that researchers use when they try to understand why adult psychopaths or children at risk of developing psychopathy lack empathy. Let's imagine that you are observing a study where the participants are required to do a set of experimental psychology tasks. These tasks have been developed to assess how people process emotions, whether they feel empathy, if they can tell right from wrong, and to what degree they experience guilt. They are the kinds of tasks that researchers have used to get a better understanding of how individuals with high levels of psychopathic features see the world around them and how this, in turn, might help explain their behaviour. As I describe each task below, I also give you examples of findings that show how the 'psychopathic outlook' differs from that of the typical participant.

Recognizing other people's distress

First up is a task that requires participants to watch faces on the computer screen. The faces start with a neutral expression, but slowly morph into an emotional expression in a step by step animation (Figure 3). The participants are required to press a button when they think they can recognize what emotion the face is showing. They get a choice of emotion words (e.g. fearful, sad, happy, and angry) and they indicate their answer.

Most of us find happy expressions very easy to identify. Fearful expressions, on the other hand, are more complicated to pick up. But we are competent at this task. Emotional facial expressions communicate important things to humans. They indicate whether

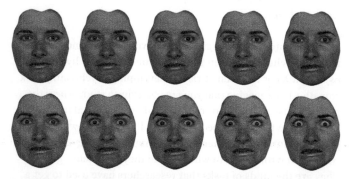

3. Stills from a task that continuously 'morphs' a face from neutral (0 per cent) to emotional (100 per cent) expression. The example emotion here is fear, which individuals with or at risk of developing psychopathy have difficulty recognizing.

someone is a threat to us, whether they welcome us or whether there is something in the environment that we should run away from. It is not a surprise that, as a species, we pay attention to emotions and read them well. Individuals with high levels of psychopathic features find a task that requires identification of emotions a lot more difficult than their peers, especially when they have to recognize other people's distress (e.g. fear). In other words, while you and I readily pick up the signs of someone being scared, individuals with high levels of psychopathic traits require the face in this task to morph closer to the full expression before they get it right.

Data from tasks like this point to slower and more error prone recognition of other people's distress in adult psychopaths and children at risk of developing the condition. This difficulty in recognizing other people's distress is also picked up with tasks that use auditory or body posture cues of emotion. Interestingly, the fact that individuals with high levels of psychopathic features do not readily pick up on others' distress also means that they can perform some other cognitive operations more efficiently than the rest of us. If you or I were doing a task that demands attention, but we detected a distressed person in the periphery, we would be enormously distracted and it would be hard for us to continue to pay attention to the task at hand. This is not just because we see a person (other people are typically interesting to humans!), but in particular because we see a person in distress (well-controlled experiments have shown that a fearful face grabs the attention more readily than a calm face).

But this is not so for a person with high levels of psychopathic features. They can continue with their attention-demanding activity just as well whether a distressed or a calm individual pops up in the periphery. In other words, they can be better at laboratory tasks that require attention and concentration because they are not affected by emotions (the same process may also explain why they can effectively focus on goals that are important to themselves, even if the pursuit of these goals is causing distress to those around them). For the rest of us, our ability to react fast in a task that demands attention is compromised, and we slow down as our concentration is broken.

Resonating with other people's distress

For the second task the participants are shown photographs of people in various degrees of distress. They may look sad or fearful to a different extent, or they may look quite calm and neutral, even happy. After viewing each photo (see Figure 4 for an example), test participants would be asked to rate how bad, neutral, or good the photograph makes them feel—on a nine-point sliding scale that goes from 'very bad' (−4) to 'very good' (+4).

This task provides a proxy for measuring empathy, how much seeing another person in distress impacts someone and makes them feel bad. Most of us readily push the slider to the 'bad' end of the scale when we see someone else in distress, but individuals with psychopathic features appear less affected. Compared to their peers, they report feeling less bad when they see such images. They also report feeling less bad when they hear about other people's misfortune. Behaviour on these types of tasks gives us some clues regarding why individuals with psychopathy are capable of hurting other people. For most of us, seeing another person in distress or discomfort acts as a brake for our behaviour. It is upsetting to see another person sad or scared or in pain, and we are likely to try to make amends. We are distressed by the hurt we have caused. If this brake on behaviour is absent or muted, it is possible to more readily pursue your own goals at the expense of other people.

Deciding what is the right thing to do—and why

In this third task, a number of short scenarios are described to the participants and they are asked some follow-up questions. I will give you examples of the kinds of scenarios here:

Scenario A: 'Boris walks up to another boy and hits him in
            the face.'
Scenario B: 'Jeremy talks to his friend while the teacher is
            speaking.'

4. An example of stimuli used in the task that tests the ability to
resonate with other people's emotions. The participants rate how
seeing the photograph makes them feel.

I would first ask the participants whether it is acceptable to act in a way described in the scenario (Yes/No). Provided that they say 'No' (most people do, even those with high levels of psychopathic traits), I would then prompt them to give me a justification regarding why it is not acceptable to act in a way described in the scenario. Finally, I would probe whether they think it would be OK to act in a way described in the scenario if there were no rules against it or if an authority figure (e.g. teacher) gave permission for the behaviour.

This deceptively simple task with short fictional scenarios gives us a lot of interesting information about how individuals with psychopathic features view the world. First, they have no difficulty in discerning that the scenarios like those described above are wrong. Just like their peers, they say it is not 'right' for Boris to hit the other boy or for Jeremy to speak to his friend in class. However, things get interesting when we ask them to provide justification for not finding the actions in the scenarios permissible.

Typically, people discuss the wrongness of moral scenarios (such as Scenario A) in terms of the potential hurt that they cause other people, i.e. 'It is wrong for Boris to hit the other boy, because the other boy will get hurt', and the wrongness of conventional scenarios (such as Scenario B) in terms of the actions being against the rules, i.e. 'It is wrong for Jeremy to speak in the class because it is against the school rules'. Individuals with high levels of psychopathic features, both adults and children, do not tend to refer to someone getting hurt (e.g. the presence of a victim) as a reason not to do something. They usually state that both types of scenarios are wrong because they are 'against the rules'.

Another interesting pattern emerges when we ask people to imagine there being no rules against the action or when we suggest that an authority figure has permitted the action. Most people still say that the moral action (Scenario A) is wrong, but now permit the conventional action (Scenario B). Individuals with psychopathic features continue to insist that both actions are wrong. On the surface, it may seem like they are displaying higher moral standards by endorsing 'good' behaviour on all occasions. However, what their answer demonstrates is that they do not make a distinction between actions that are bad regardless of rules and those which are permissible (and will not hurt others) if the rules are removed. And, perhaps more tellingly, despite 'knowing the rules' and giving a socially acceptable answer regarding transgressions being 'wrong', they repeatedly behave in ways that hurt and upset other people and break societal norms.

This gives us a clue that it is not enough to know what is right or wrong, it is also critically important to 'feel it'. Feeling for other people's distress, finding it upsetting, is what researchers think is a key motivator of moral behaviour. As I mentioned before, we can think of this propensity to take in others' distress and find it upsetting as the 'brakes' that stop most people from hurting others. And we know from tasks that assess the ability to resonate with other people's emotions that individuals with high levels of psychopathic traits do not have such brakes in a fully functioning order.

Ability to feel guilt

This brings me to the fourth and final task of the imaginary testing session. In this task I would present participants with everyday scenarios and ask them to picture themselves as the main character in them. The scenarios describe situations where the participant will either inconvenience or harm another person or situations that inconvenience or harm them personally. In both cases the content of the scenario is emotive, but in only one case—where there is potential for another person to be harmed—feelings of guilt should arise. Consider these two examples.

Scenario A. 'You are hoping for a promotion in your job. During a meeting, your team manager praises the team's work. He is very complimentary about a novel idea the team has introduced. He says the idea was yours. You know it was not; it was your colleague's. But you don't say anything because you don't want to risk your promotion.'

Scenario B. 'You are hoping for a promotion in your job. During a meeting, your team manager praises the team's work. He is very complimentary about a novel idea the team has introduced. He says the idea was your colleague's. You know it was your idea but you don't say anything because you don't want to risk your promotion.'

Most people report feeling guilt in relation to scenarios where another person is likely to experience hurt or disadvantage as a direct result of their (the protagonist's) actions (like Scenario A). The scenarios involving personal hurt (like Scenario B) are reported as equally emotionally negative, but people do not report feeling guilt in relation to these scenarios. If your actions and choices harm you, you feel bad, but you do not feel guilty. Individuals with high levels of psychopathic traits report feeling less guilty than their peers in response to scenarios that involve harm to others and that typically evoke guilt.

A number of studies on adult and child samples that use different tasks to prod individuals' ability to feel guilt report similar findings. Those with high levels of psychopathic features do not feel guilty in the same way as the rest of us. However, they feel just as annoyed as everyone else when they, the 'number one', are disadvantaged, inconvenienced, or miss out on something. This means that any findings related to reported feelings of guilt cannot be explained by a wholesale inability to feel negative emotions. Psychopaths can and do feel bad and frustrated when *their* needs are not fully met. They just do not feel keenly for other people's misfortune or for their role in causing that misfortune.

What have experimental studies shown us?

Experimental studies, such as those described above, have collectively shown us that individuals with psychopathic traits do not find other people's distress as important and do not resonate with it as readily as other people do. Some of these studies have recorded the degree of participants' physiological arousal, such as skin conductance, in response to other people's distress.

Skin conductance quantifies changes in the skin's resistance that occur when sweat glands in the skin produce more or less sweat and can be measured by placing small electrodes on the fingertips. The more aroused someone is, as people are for instance when they are upset or excited, the more their skin sweats. Studies utilizing skin conductance measures have shown that individuals with high levels of psychopathy do not find witnessing other people's distress as physiologically arousing as their peers do.

In short, while the rest of us appear to automatically and effortlessly compute other people's upset and feel bad about it, those with psychopathic features are operating on a muted dial. The failure to feel for others or to feel bad when contemplating one's own behaviour means that when they are focused on looking after 'number one', individuals with psychopathic features can violate the rights of other people with ease and fail to apply the brakes to their antisocial behaviour. They lack the intrinsic motivation to consider other people's feelings and avoid harming others, which may explain why they behave in morally dubious ways despite knowing right from wrong.

Are individuals with psychopathy on the autism spectrum?

Sometimes people are confused and say: 'But individuals with autism lack empathy, what is the difference between autism and psychopathy?' Behaviours can at times look similar on the surface.

This is why it is important to conduct carefully designed experimental research that can elucidate whether the behaviour is related to similar or different information-processing biases. Studies that have systematically compared and contrasted individuals with high levels of psychopathic vs. autistic features have helped us to understand crucial differences between social information processing associated with these conditions.

The primary problem for individuals on the autism spectrum is not the inability to feel for others, but the profound difficulty in reading other people's minds and consequently behaving in a socially appropriate manner. This means that individuals on the autism spectrum can come across as if they lack empathy, but in fact many of them report that they feel deeply for other people's and animals' misfortune.

A friend who is on the autism spectrum tells me that she often finds situations where she witnesses other people in distress emotionally overwhelming and has to leave, particularly as she is not sure that she would be able to 'say the right thing'. Individuals with psychopathy do not suffer from such concerns. My friend's anecdote is backed up by empirical data. Research by my own group and other scientists has clearly shown us that the kind of empathy deficit seen in psychopathy is very different from the difficulties shown by individuals on the autism spectrum.

In a number of studies of both children and adults we have given participants tasks where they need to report how much they resonate with other people's emotions, how much they care about other people's misfortunes, or how well they understand other people's thoughts and motivations. Compared with typical, healthy 'control' individuals, those with high levels of psychopathic traits resonate less with other people's emotions and care less about other people's misfortunes. However, they do not differ from healthy controls in their ability to understand other people's thoughts and motivations: they are able to perform so-called 'theory of mind' computations. Individuals on the autism spectrum present the opposite way. Compared with healthy controls they have difficulties in tasks that require theory of mind computations, but do not differ from healthy controls in the degree to which they resonate with other people's emotions or care about their misfortunes.

In short, individuals with psychopathy do not resonate with other people's emotions, but they are perfectly able to work out what other people are thinking—especially when doing so benefits them. They are often skilled manipulators. By contrast, individuals on the autism spectrum, as a rule, find it distressing to witness other people's negative emotions (they show physiological arousal to other's distress), but are not known for their ability to deftly manipulate other people—which makes sense if you have difficulty in computing what other people are thinking and if you care about others' distress.

I do not doubt that some people on the autism spectrum have substantial behavioural problems, and that we can find individuals on the autism spectrum who have criminal records. There is also a fascinating, small group of individuals who score highly on psychopathic and autism spectrum features and who have difficulty in tasks that assess resonating with other people's emotions, as well as tasks that require working out what other people are thinking. But overall we do not see the heightened risk for criminality in individuals on the autism spectrum (their rates of criminality look similar to the general population rates of criminality), whereas those with high levels of psychopathic features are definitely at an increased risk of antisocial and criminal conduct.

If individuals with psychopathy are able to understand other minds, why do they so often appear utterly oblivious to other people's needs? Some interesting new data from Dr Arielle

Baskin-Sommers's group at Yale University suggest that psychopaths may only deploy their theory of mind skills when they want something from other people; otherwise they appear not to think about what is on other people's minds as spontaneously as you or I would. Dr Baskin-Sommers and her colleague Professor Joe Newman from the University of Wisconsin have studied how psychopathic criminals perform in tasks that require them to pay attention. Their work shows that these individuals are less distracted when they pursue task goals than their peers. Perhaps individuals with psychopathy only expend resources towards paying attention and thinking about other people if there is something in it for themselves? Otherwise they will utterly focus on the pursuit of their own goals.

'Unempathetic brains'

It would be very peculiar if the brains of people who behave differently and process information differently looked entirely typical. There is no behaviour or cognition without the brain—ergo, if behaviour or the way that information is processed is unusual, it is probable that the brain is not entirely 'mainstream' either. Several studies of adult criminal psychopaths and children at risk of developing psychopathy have reported differences in the structure of the brain areas associated with emotion processing and empathy, including the amygdala, anterior insula, anterior cingulate cortex, and inferior frontal gyrus (Figure 5). Psychopathic features in community samples are also related to differences in these brain regions.

Brain-imaging techniques, such as functional magnetic resonance imaging, can be used to study not only the brain structure but also the 'brain in action'. Studies using functional magnetic resonance imaging (fMRI) technology show what brain areas are engaged when an individual processes particular types of information. Such research provides us with information that complements the findings from cognitive experimental studies.

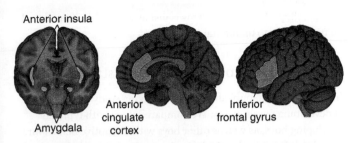

Anterior insula

Amygdala

Anterior cingulate cortex

Inferior frontal gyrus

5. The amygdala, anterior insula, anterior cingulate cortex, and inferior frontal gyrus. The amygdala is a subcortical region that is important for processing the current value of stimuli and has a critical role in several affective processes, such as mediating conditioned emotional responses, responding to various emotional stimuli (including facial expressions of emotion), and in social behaviour towards conspecifics. The anterior insula plays an important role in sensory integration and interoceptive awareness and may be involved in awareness of unpleasant feelings during empathy for pain. The anterior cingulate cortex is thought to play a distinct role in complex aspects of emotion, such as processing moral emotions (e.g. guilt), empathy, self-regulation of negative emotions, and action reinforcement (route by which reward history influences action choice). The inferior frontal gyrus is important for experiencing emotional contagion, in other words resonance with other people's emotions. These brain areas often work together to process emotionally significant information.

So what goes on in the brains of psychopaths, and how might finding out help us further understand their behaviour? Neuroimaging studies have been conducted on criminal psychopaths, on children at risk of developing psychopathy, and on community samples of adults with varying levels of psychopathic traits. Collectively these studies yield a relatively consistent picture of underactivity in brain areas that are involved in processing other people's distress and pain, empathy, and guilt. By contrast, brain activity related to theory of mind computations that do not require deciphering emotions—in other words, brain activity related to understanding other people's minds and motivations—appears entirely normal in individuals with psychopathic features. This is just as we would expect based on their ability to manipulate others.

Brain responses to other people's distress

In 2012 my group published a neuroimaging study of boys at risk of developing psychopathy. We compared them with typically developing boys, as well as other boys with disruptive behaviours but who did not display the lack of empathy that is a hallmark of psychopathy. All groups were matched on age, cognitive ability, socio-economic status, and their preferred use of right or left hand (handedness can impact brain organization and we match our groups on this variable so that we can be sure it is not responsible for any group differences we might find—ditto for age, cognitive ability, and socio-economic status).

Our aim was to focus on the function of a small, almond-shaped structure buried deep inside the temporal lobe of the brain—the amygdala (Figure 6). The amygdala is a subcortical region that has a key role in processing the importance of things. It has a critical role in responding to various emotionally salient stimuli, in other words stimuli that we should notice and pay attention to. Such stimuli include facial expressions of emotion, and the amygdala responds to them, even when we do not consciously perceive seeing an emotion. It is thought that this rapid response to important things in our environment helps us orient towards things that we should not miss, such as signals from our fellow human beings that they may need help or that there may be danger in the environment.

When the boys were inside the fMRI scanner we gave them a very simple task to probe their amygdala function. They were asked to lie still and view faces that were presented very rapidly. For every facial identity that the participants perceived, they were in fact presented with two faces of different identities. The first face, which had either a fearful or a calm expression, was presented

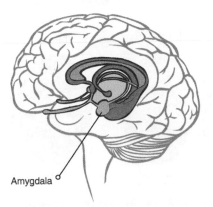

Amygdala

6. The amygdala (Latin, *corpus amygdaloideum*), an almond-shaped set of neurons located deep in the brain's medial temporal lobe. It has a key role in alerting us to significant things in our surroundings, including other people's distress.

very rapidly for only 17 milliseconds. It was then replaced by another face, a calm one of a different identity, that remained on the screen for further 183 milliseconds (Figure 7 shows what the task looked like).

This procedure is called 'backward masking', and the study participants only perceive the face they see for 183 milliseconds, not the one that preceded it for 17 milliseconds. This task enables us to get a snapshot of how the boys' brains respond to emotional faces, even when these are not consciously perceived. The participants did not realize there were two faces or that they saw emotional faces (we checked). However, we did see differences in how the brains of the different groups of boys reacted to the emotional faces that they did not consciously perceive.

The boys at risk of developing psychopathy showed the lowest amygdala response to backward masked fear. The boys with disruptive behaviour (but who did not lack empathy) showed the highest amygdala response to backward masked fear. The typically

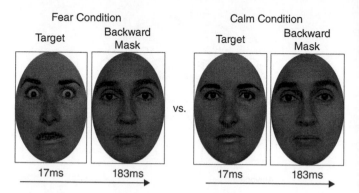

Fear Condition | Calm Condition

Target | Backward Mask | Target | Backward Mask

17ms | 183ms | 17ms | 183ms

vs.

7. **The backward mask task. We compare brain activity to subliminally presented fearful and calm faces. Boys at risk of developing psychopathy showed diminished amygdala response to the fear faces.**

developing boys showed amygdala activity that was somewhere in the middle of these two groups. These findings were exciting as they showed us very clearly that signals of other people's distress are not salient for boys at risk of developing psychopathy, their brains are not attuned to fear as something that needs to be noted.

What was also clear from our study was that this presentation is unique to them, rather than universal among all boys with disruptive behaviours. In fact, those with disruptive behaviours but the ability to empathize looked atypical in exactly the opposite way to boys at risk of developing psychopathy. Their brains were overresponsive rather than underresponsive to other people's distress. These findings very much accord with the experimental data that show that boys at risk of developing psychopathy do not readily resonate with other people's emotions.

Brain responses to other people's pain

In 2013 Professor Jean Decety, Professor Kent Kiehl, and their colleagues reported findings on a sample of incarcerated individuals who had been scanned while watching pictures of body parts in painful situations. They were instructed to either imagine themselves or other people in the situations depicted by the pictures. When inmates with high levels of psychopathic traits were told to imagine themselves in the pictures, they showed increased activity in the anterior insula, anterior cingulate cortex, and inferior frontal gyrus—compared with inmates who had low levels of psychopathic traits. In other words, they readily engaged brain areas that are known to be involved in processing salient information and responding to and introspecting about emotional states when they were required to consider 'number one' in a painful situation.

However, when they were asked to imagine another person in the pictures, inmates with high levels of psychopathic traits (as compared with those who had low levels of such traits) showed reduced response in, and connectivity between, these brain areas. In other words, brain areas that are involved in indexing salience, and responding to and introspecting about emotion, were not engaged effectively when inmates with high levels of psychopathic traits imagined other people in painful situations. This pattern of brain activity was particularly associated with the psychopathy symptoms that indexed lack of empathy and grandiose sense of self-worth. Those individuals who had most of these symptoms had the lowest brain responses to another person's pain.

We gave a similar task to boys at risk of developing psychopathy in work led by my former PhD student Patricia Lockwood, and found muted brain responses to other people's pain—similar to those reported by Decety, Kiehl, and colleagues. This pattern of weak neural response to other people's suffering may help explain psychopaths' callous behaviour towards others, despite the suffering that such behaviour causes. It may also contribute to the uncanny ability of psychopaths to focus on 'number one' at the expense of others.

Brain responses to moral evaluations and guilt

Neuroimaging research can also help us understand why seemingly typical moral judgements are not associated with typical moral behaviour in individuals with psychopathy. A number of studies of adult psychopaths have shown that although they are able to make appropriate moral judgements (deciding that an action is wrong), they use different brain areas to make these decisions than typical adults or other incarcerated inmates who do not have psychopathy. They are less likely to engage brain regions important for processing emotions and more likely to engage brain regions important for reasoning and cognitive control when they engage in moral decision making. This means that they use different cognitive operations, brain computations if you like, when they process morally relevant information. They are less likely to rely on emotional responses to the possible suffering of others, perhaps understandably if those responses are very muted, and are more likely to use cold reasoning to arrive at a judgement of what is the 'right' and what is the 'wrong' thing to do. This may explain why, although they know right from wrong, that does not necessarily guide their behaviour. They do not seem to 'feel it'. A boy with psychopathic traits whom I saw when I was conducting my PhD research had demonstrated a clear understanding of right and wrong in our tests. During the testing session he also boasted that he had recently beaten up another boy and stolen his money. I asked him whether he considered this to be wrong. He replied: 'Yes, it's against the rules, but I did not get caught and losers are there to be used.'

A recent study by our group points to moral feeling being a key motivator of moral behaviour. We know that the anterior insula is engaged when people introspect about emotions. A study by my former PhD student Ana Seara-Cardoso indicated that the degree to which the anterior insula responds to anticipated guilt varies as a function of psychopathic features. Those with the highest levels of psychopathic traits activate this region least when they process scenarios that typically evoke guilt (such as those described earlier). This finding suggests the anticipation of guilt is attenuated in those with high levels of psychopathic traits. Importantly, we showed that this pattern was specific to neural responses to anticipated feelings of guilt, and not linked to moral judgements. Our data are in line with the idea that individuals with high levels of psychopathic traits may not lack the ability to compute moral judgements per se, but instead fail to generate the distressing moral emotions that usually inhibit harmful actions towards others, such as anticipated guilt.

What we still need to know

Perhaps one of the reasons that psychopaths find it difficult to resonate with other people's distress is that distress emotions are relatively alien to them. If you do not feel something yourself, it is difficult to fully orient to and empathize with that feeling in others. For example, if you are not regularly distressed yourself, why would you be able to automatically resonate with other people's distress? This also means that you may not automatically project the consequences of your behaviour in a way that evokes feelings of guilt. In this situation, what is there to hold you back if you want to look after 'number one'?

Findings from interviews and questionnaires indeed suggest that individuals with high levels of psychopathic features may be less prone to feeling distress or fear themselves. Criminal psychopaths often comment on distressing events not having the same impact on them as they do on other people. They may boast about violence they have committed and how they felt nothing for the victims. I have also had prisoners recall laughing at people when they were scared. More than once I have had an inmate express contempt for their peers who are 'weak', emotional, scared, and 'care too much for other people'. They have expressed pride in not being affected by emotions, which means that they can get on with achieving their goals (even if this means seriously hurting another person). Children at risk of developing psychopathy also report this.

We need more systematic research into the origins of empathy deficits in psychopathy and whether it is possible for them to develop a spontaneous and reliable empathetic response to help motivate moral behaviour. Could this improve our chances of helping people like Mark? I will return to this theme in Chapters 4 and 5, where I consider the development and treatment of psychopathy.

Chapter 3
Explaining impulsivity and failure to behave prosocially

Lack of empathy for distress helps explain why psychopaths have no difficulty in engaging in premeditated hurtful and antisocial behaviour. But it does not fully explain the behavioural profile of individuals with psychopathy. Why do psychopaths often make foolish life choices that are likely to result in serious repercussions to them? Why don't they worry about other people's happiness and establish loving relationships?

Both Mark and David, in different ways, have clearly made decisions that are risky and poorly thought out. Mark has got caught committing crimes several times and although David has managed to avoid a legal case so far, he has engaged in serious deception and blackmailing that could cost him his career. Neither of our case studies is concerned about other people's well-being or loyalty. It is evident that lack of empathy and guilt do not account for all aspects of psychopathic behaviour—other factors are at play too.

When sanctions don't bite, but rewards look very promising

One remarkable feature of adult criminal psychopaths, as well as children at risk of developing psychopathy, is the fact that they often make poorly thought out, impulsive decisions—much more commonly than their peers—which then result in unpleasant repercussions not just for other people, but also for themselves. Most people are deterred from risky and antisocial behaviours in part because they worry about the consequences.

Individuals with psychopathy seem quite willing to take risks in order to get something that they want, even if there is a strong likelihood of reprisal. This was very evident to me when I was collecting data in prisons at the very start of my research career. I read hundreds of prison files that detailed the inmates' backgrounds and offences and what always struck me was the sheer foolishness of some of the decisions that individuals with psychopathy made, time and again, despite the consequences. I was at a loss to explain how they thought the risk was worth it, particularly when the consequences were, to my mind, out of kilter with the potential gains.

Examples of spectacularly bad decisions included robbing a corner shop with CCTV cameras while on parole, just to get a few beers and a modest amount of cash; a decision to go joyriding on a stolen motorbike, a few weeks after release from prison; and repeatedly engaging in fights despite the fact that such behaviour had often resulted in a conviction previously. Why did these men make such poor decisions? I could understand that their personality meant that they did not care about the consequences of their actions to other people, but it was a mystery to me why individuals who were clearly very motivated to look after their own needs often made choices that really disadvantaged them.

Research using tasks that measure how individuals learn from punishments and rewards has shown that compared with peers of similar age and educational background, individuals with psychopathy appear insensitive to punishments and atypically focused on rewards. They take longer to learn about bad options and seem more surprised and frustrated by the negative consequences of their actions. It is as if they are not really able to anticipate something going wrong when they focus on something that they really want. Individuals with psychopathy also seem to experience some sanctions as less aversive than their peers. In other words, sanctions may not have quite the same 'bite' as they do for the rest of us.

Classic experimental studies in the field have shown, time and again, that both adult psychopaths and children at risk of developing psychopathy have difficulty learning from punishments and often keep on making decisions that are not in their best interest. This is of course evident from accounts of their everyday behaviour, but the experimental tasks offer a way of formalizing what information processing (i.e. cognitive) biases may account for the everyday behaviour that we see. If they are given an experimental task that requires them to learn what stimuli regularly lose them points and what stimuli are 'safer', individuals with psychopathy take a longer time to learn the distinction between safe and unsafe options than their peers. They are also worse at spotting that the likelihood of something being rewarding has changed. In tasks where stimuli are first rewarded with points but then become 'unsafe' and start losing points, learning this reversal in fortunes takes much longer for individuals with high levels of psychopathic traits than it does for their peers.

More recent work by Professor James Blair and other colleagues has used so-called computational modelling methods to characterize the specific aspects of information processing that are 'off' in those individuals with high levels of psychopathic features when they make decisions. These sorts of models enable scientists to not only demonstrate that someone learns more slowly about punishments and rewards, but also helps them to pinpoint why.

Computational modelling experiments have shown that individuals with high levels of psychopathic traits make so-called 'prediction errors'. In other words their predictions about outcomes of their choices are often wrong. Such experiments have also demonstrated that they compute 'expected value' differently from their peers. In other words, their expectations of an outcome are not accurate. Psychophysiological experiments that measure arousal, for example via skin conductance (which is essentially the changes in sweating that occur when we feel nervous or excited), have also shown that arousal responses to impending negative outcomes can be muted in individuals with psychopathy. This may be in part because they are simply not processing all of the relevant information about punishments or losses as fully as their peers.

Poorer ability to predict likely punishments can help explain why individuals with psychopathy keep on making poor decisions, even when such decisions have resulted in undesirable outcomes in the past. If their anticipation of consequences is less accurate and their focus on the potential reward is unusually myopic, then they are making their decisions based on different information than most people. In other words the signals guiding the decision making of a psychopath and a non-psychopath are not the same.

As I alluded to in Chapter 2, psychopaths can be extremely focused on their own goals, paying attention only to those aspects of the world that they deem relevant for what they need. We might say that the way in which they process possible punishments and rewards, and their subsequent predictions about the world around them, are 'skewed'. It is easy to see how atypical processing of punishment information, and difficulties in anticipating punishment, combined with undue focus on rewards, may lead to decision making that is not optimal and gets the psychopath into trouble.

Do individuals with psychopathy have punishment insensitive brains?

Brain-imaging studies have shown that the regions associated with processing reinforcement information (i.e. information about rewards and punishments), including the striatum and ventromedial prefrontal cortex, function atypically in adults with psychopathy and children at risk of developing psychopathy. This is unsurprising. Differences in decision making must have their seat in how the brain processes information. For example, work by Dr Joshua Buckholtz's group from Harvard has shown that higher levels of psychopathic features in incarcerated adults are associated with stronger brain activation to rewards in the striatum. He has also demonstrated that individuals with the highest levels of psychopathy have the poorest connectivity (we can think of this as two brain areas talking to each other) between striatum and ventromedial prefrontal cortex. The ventromedial prefrontal cortex is thought to be involved in representing value and has an impact on choice behaviour by modulating striatal signals about rewards. Effective 'communication' between ventromedial prefrontal cortex and striatum is therefore critical for adapting behaviour in response to expected outcomes. If this communication is disrupted, in particular if and when rewards appear, that is likely to lead to poor choices.

To study whether this is the case for psychopaths, Dr Buckholtz and colleagues related their brain connectivity data to criminal conviction records. They showed that the pattern of atypical brain connections that was seen in participants with high levels of psychopathic features predicted the number of subsequent criminal convictions. In other words, the neural underpinnings of poor decision making were not only related to the performance on the experimental decision-making task that the inmates undertook in the scanner when they were participating in Dr Buckholtz's study, but also related to their real-life decision making.

Atypical reinforcement signalling in the ventromedial prefrontal cortex, as well as differences in ventromedial prefrontal cortex–striatal connectivity, are also seen in the brains of children and adolescents at risk of developing psychopathy. This suggests that the atypical cognitive and neural processes associated with decision making are unlikely to simply reflect long histories of antisocial behaviour and substance abuse, but may indicate intrinsic vulnerability to psychopathic and antisocial lifestyle.

Why should we care about understanding how individuals with psychopathy process reinforcement information?

Individuals with psychopathy are not unique in having difficulties in reinforcement learning and optimal decision making. Other individuals with antisocial behaviour and impulse control disorders also have difficulty in this domain. However, having this particular cognitive bias may be especially destructive in individuals with psychopathy as they are more poised to look after number one than anyone else and also care less about the consequences of their poor decision making for other people. In other words, being poor at computing the consequences of your actions is particularly toxic when you also lack empathy for other people's distress. Not getting what you want, or not being able to predict what will happen as a consequence of your choices, can also result in extreme frustration, aggression, and anger in individuals with psychopathy. They typically blame others for their mistakes and fail to see how their own actions contributed to the negative consequences. Instead they often view such consequences as disproportionate, or a mistake altogether—not something that they deserve.

We know that people's behaviour is not just motivated by the desire to avoid sanctions. People are also very keen on rewards. In fact, rewarding good behaviour with something concrete such as a special treat, or with praise, often gets better results than threatening people with sanctions, regardless of whether they have high levels of psychopathic features or not. Individuals with psychopathy certainly seem motivated by some rewards. They care about their own pleasure and material gains, and they can pursue what they want while ignoring the potential negative consequences, as we have just learned.

This focus on rewards can both spell trouble and also offer hope. If left unchecked, being driven by rewards, not computing the potential repercussions of certain behaviours, and not worrying about other people's distress can lead a person to selfishly fulfil their desires without any concern for other people's needs. On the other hand, it might be possible to harness the responsivity to material rewards to motivate good behaviour, 'looking after number one in prosocial ways' if you like. I will return to this theme in Chapter 5 where I discuss possible interventions for adults with psychopathy and children at risk of developing the disorder.

What about social rewards?

Right now I want to spend some time considering yet another puzzling aspect of psychopathic presentation—their seeming lack of interest in pleasing and bringing joy to other people and their inability (or lack of desire) to form deep, loving, affiliative relationships. It is as if psychopaths are able to get excited about material rewards, but do not find social relationships rewarding and motivating in the same way as the rest of us do.

As a rule, all group-living animals, including humans, have a basic urge to affiliate with members of their own species. People are prosocial creatures. We typically form enduring bonds with others. We find spending time with our family and friends rewarding, we rejoice in their good fortune, we want to help them and often go to a substantial degree of bother for others. This applies particularly in relation to people whom we consider to be part of our 'in group', but also often in relation to strangers. People give to charity, give up a seat in a crowded train for the elderly, and call an ambulance when someone is injured. We are usually loyal and we do not betray those that we work or live with.

One of the striking hallmarks of individuals with psychopathy (or those at risk of developing the condition) is that their relationships seem shallow, transient, and transactional. Several empirical studies indicate that they show reduced quality of attachment in peer, romantic, and work relationships. For example, compared with individuals with low levels of psychopathic traits, the peer relationships of those with high levels of psychopathic features are characterized by lack of stability, their marital relationships are less harmonious, and they are perceived as being less reliable team players in the workplace. They often treat people as dispensable, and are charming and nice only when it is in their clear self-interest. They do not appear to be distressed by conflicts in relationships and report preferring one-night stands to committed relationships. Why do individuals with psychopathy not show typical prosocial and affiliative behaviours that characterize humans on the whole? Remarkably, there has been very little work systematically investigating this question.

Atypical experience of social reward?

Psychopaths' behaviour indicates they may have an atypical experience of social reward. Social reward can be defined as the motivational and pleasurable aspects of our interactions with other people. For example, being kind and having close relationships with others is fundamentally rewarding for most people, but perhaps not so for individuals with high levels of psychopathic features. These individuals are antagonistic. They report placing less importance on kindness to others and affiliative, long-term friendships and relationships. We can see this in studies that have focused on surveying real-life behaviour in friendships, romantic relationships, and in the workplace. It is also in evidence in more formal experimental tasks that measure cooperation with others. When doing these sorts of tasks, individuals with high levels of psychopathic traits are less likely to cooperate with and help others. Experimental studies also indicate that individuals with psychopathy may find paying attention to others less rewarding.

Reading this research got my former PhD student Lucy Foulkes and me interested in whether people with high levels of psychopathic traits find affiliative and prosocial behaviour towards others less rewarding than the rest of us. We also wondered whether they might find some nasty behaviours more rewarding than their peers. Prior research had shown that they enjoy antisocial entertainments such as violent sports and video games and also engage in internet 'trolling'.

Together with a colleague, Professor Craig Neumann from the University of North Texas, Lucy and I developed an instrument to assess different aspects of social reward in adults and adolescents. Lucy called the instrument the Social Reward Questionnaire and, after validating it, she administered this measure alongside assessment of psychopathic traits in both adult and adolescent samples. As we had predicted, individuals with high levels of psychopathic traits reported enjoying prosocial actions less and nasty/dominating behaviours towards others more than their peers. We were not surprised by these findings. Both we and colleagues had regularly observed the kinds of behaviours that would suggest that the motivation for the social behaviour of individuals with high levels of psychopathic traits is unlikely to be similar to what motivates social behaviour for the rest of us. But our findings formalized the 'hunch' that we had before.

The finding that individuals with high levels of psychopathic traits appeared to enjoy cruel interactions have prompted people to wonder about a connection between psychopathy and sadism. Sadism is defined as the enjoyment of controlling, dominating, and/or causing suffering to others, and can refer to physical or psychological suffering. Empirical studies have shown that there is a reliable, but modest, association between psychopathy and sadism (not all psychopaths are sadists and not all sadists are psychopaths). What we do not yet know is why some individuals with high levels of psychopathic traits enjoy cruel behaviour. Is there something inherently pleasurable in causing another person pain (physical or psychological)? And why would this be the case? Perhaps the answer lies in what another person's pain can signify.

Lucy and I speculated that the enjoyment may stem from the power and control that comes with inflicting suffering, and it is this rather than the pain per se that has reward value. In other words, the other person's pain signals that you have achieved a goal, the person is under your control and you can use that person to fulfil your own needs. Of course some individuals with psychopathy may also enjoy inflicting suffering.

We also found that high levels of psychopathic traits were associated with reduced enjoyment of prosocial interactions. This finding suggests that individuals with high levels of psychopathic traits do not just feel indifferent towards being kind and helpful, they find it unappealing. Except, perhaps, when there is something in it for them. Research conducted prior to our own study has shown that individuals with high levels of psychopathic traits are prone to exaggerating their good deeds when they think that this will be good for their image, but report less prosocial and altruistic behaviour when they do not stand to benefit from doing things for others. This is in stark contrast to most people who report that they find helping others rewarding in and of itself and do not only engage in prosocial behaviours when this has an instrumental benefit to them.

What could explain the differences in what individuals with psychopathy and their peers find socially rewarding? The answer is not likely to be simple and there is a lot we do not yet know. But we are trying to find pieces to this part of the puzzle. Here I want to give a few examples of how we can assess cognitive processes that are thought to promote social affiliation and group cohesion and systematically investigate whether individuals with psychopathic traits look different. So far the majority of this work has focused on children at risk of developing psychopathy.

Unexpected 'happy' discovery

One of the ways in which we can assess whether something is inherently salient is to see how well it captures our attention. If I gave you an experimental task of attention where you had to view three faces, one male and two females, appearing on the screen at the same time (see Figure 8a and 8b) and asked you to indicate whether the male face is tilted to the left or right, you could pick this out quite quickly (typically well under one second). However, if any of the three faces displayed emotion, this would usually affect the speed of doing the task and you would slow down. Not by seconds, but by several tens and in some cases hundreds of milliseconds. This is because emotions signal that there is something important in the environment, something worth paying attention to, and we cannot help but process them.

This is exactly what we see in the case of typically developing children. However, not so for boys at risk of developing psychopathy. My former PhD student Sara Hodsoll used an attentional capture task, like the one I have just described, and demonstrated that seeing emotional faces does not capture the attention of children at risk of developing psychopathy.

When we started our data collection, we were interested in the ability of other people's distress (fear) to capture the attention of boys at risk of developing psychopathy and included happy faces simply so that the participants would have something positive to view. As predicted, we demonstrated that fearful faces did not capture the attention of boys at risk of developing psychopathy. This was in line with other research that had demonstrated atypical fear processing in psychopathy. We did not expect any

8. The attentional capture task. Participants detect a male face in a display of one male and two female faces. They then indicate whether the male face is tilted left or right. This task can be used to test whether the presence of an emotional expression, e.g. happiness (8a) is distracting and captures attention (as indicated by a longer reaction time). Trials with an emotional face can be compared with trials where all faces are neutral and there are no distracting emotional expressions (8b). Boys at risk of developing psychopathy are not distracted by emotional faces.

differences in how happy faces were processed, but to our surprise these faces also did not distract boys at risk of developing psychopathy.

Around the time that we published our finding, our colleague Dr Kostas Fanti from the University of Cyprus also reported atypical neural activation patterns to happy faces in children at risk of developing psychopathy, using functional near-infrared spectroscopy to chart brain activity. The unexpected 'happy findings' led us to wonder whether very basic social stimuli that promote affiliation and closeness with other humans are not processed in a typical way by individuals with high levels of psychopathic traits.

Positive social stimuli such as happy faces or genuine laughter are potent, universal signals that promote social bonds, mutual liking, and pleasure. We find these signals distracting, contagious, and rewarding. Yet, perhaps individuals with psychopathy or those at risk of developing the condition do not experience them in this way? While we have learned a great deal from our and other researchers' work on negative emotions, particularly in relation to risk for aggression, we know remarkably little about the processes underlying the atypical social affiliation in individuals with psychopathy. This is surprising, given the importance of social affiliation and bonding in promoting social order and reducing aggression. Many of the neurocognitive mechanisms that subserve empathy for distress may also be involved in processing positive affective/affiliative cues that promote social cohesion and bonding. Laughter seemed like an interesting probe to further test the hypothesis that the processing of affiliative signals is atypical in individuals with psychopathic features.

Laughter

Laughter is a universal expression of emotion used to maintain social bonds. It is highly contagious: it can be primed simply by listening to others' laughter. Such emotional contagion has been posited as a mechanism for facilitating the coupling of emotions and behaviour within groups, increasing cooperation, cohesiveness, and social connectedness. The social nature of laughter is nicely demonstrated by the fact that an individual is up to thirty times more likely to laugh when they are with others than when they are alone. Laughter also plays a role in the vicarious experience of positive emotions, something that is thought to be key for promoting prosocial communication and social bonding in primates and other mammals.

Neuroimaging studies by my University College London (UCL) colleague Professor Sophie Scott and other researchers have shown that listening to laughter automatically recruits brain areas that are involved in the production of emotional expressions, including motor and premotor regions, the supplementary motor area, and the anterior insula. A preparatory motor response is thought to facilitate joining in with others' positive vocalizations during social behaviour, representing a neural mechanism for experiencing these emotions vicariously. This, in turn, is proposed to promote social connectedness. Research on typical individuals has established laughter as an interesting probe for examining the atypical social affiliation and connectedness that we see in individuals with or at risk of developing psychopathy.

This is precisely what two postdoctoral researchers, Dr Liz O'Nions from my group and Dr César Lima from Professor Sophie Scott's group, did. They scanned nearly a hundred boys as they listened to audio clips of laughter in the scanner. We had boys who were at risk of developing psychopathy, those who had disruptive behaviours but low levels of psychopathic traits, and typically developing boys who had similar cognitive ability and socio-economic backgrounds.

The first indication of atypical laughter processing emerged from our behavioural data. Children at risk of developing psychopathy reported that they felt less inclined to join in with other people's genuine laughter than the typically developing boys did. We did not see a difference between the other boys with disruptive behaviours and typically developing boys in their desire to join in with laughter. Our neuroimaging data were in line with the behavioural data. Boys who were at risk of developing psychopathy had reduced responses to genuine laughter in the anterior insula (see Figure 9). The anterior insula is associated with the automatic priming of motor responses elicited by emotional vocalizations, as well as with the experience of emotional and motivational aspects of laughter. Other boys with disruptive behaviours did not have anterior insula responses that clearly differed from our typically developing boys' responses. What was fascinating to us was that the reduced anterior insula responses to genuine laughter in part explained why the boys at risk of developing psychopathy reported a reduced desire to join

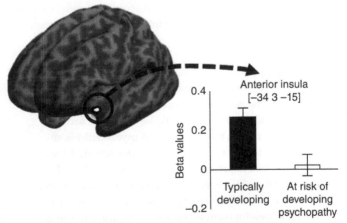

9. Comparing responses to genuine laughter in the anterior insula (beta values represent estimates of brain activity). In contrast to typically developing boys, boys who are at risk of developing psychopathy have reduced brain activity in the anterior insula when responding to genuine laughter. (Numbers in brackets [–34 3 –15] represent the precise brain coordinates of the activation.)

in with other people's genuine laughter. This suggests a link between how the anterior insula part of the brain responds and how the laughter is perceived. In the case of boys at risk of developing psychopathy, the laughter was perceived to be less motivating and inviting.

We also got the boys to listen to posed laughter when they were inside the scanner and asked them to discriminate between posed and real laughter when they were outside the scanner. We did not see any differences between any of the groups of boys in their auditory cortex responses to laughter or their ability to discriminate between posed and genuine laughter (either at the neural or behavioural level). This indicates that the group differences in responses to genuine laughter were not caused by some basic difficulties in hearing or because the boys at risk of developing psychopathy did not have the capacity to infer the social meaning of laughter. The finding that boys at risk of developing psychopathy were able to discriminate social meaning in this task is consistent with their intact ability to understand other minds.

Laughter, and positive social affiliative signals more broadly, could represent one important mechanism that—when atypical—may impoverish social relationships and increase the risk of developing psychopathy. This would be consistent with evolutionary accounts that suggest that psychopathy is an alternative strategy to mutualistic social investment driven by shared emotional experience and collaboration. It is, of course, also possible that differences in neural responses to laughter could reflect a consequence of poor social connectedness over the course of development explained by atypical parenting. Our study that only focused on the boys at a single time point cannot answer what has led to this kind of information-processing bias.

What we still need to know

We are beginning to understand why individuals with psychopathy make poor, impulsive decisions. This can help scientists design more effective interventions that encourage better decision making and some of this work is already taking place. We are also starting to unpick potential reasons for their reduced motivation to affiliate with and please others. This area needs a lot more focus and thought. For example, we need to find tasks that can be used in different age groups and which might help us study the development of atypical social affiliation longitudinally.

Chapter 4
Why do some people become psychopaths?

The findings from cognitive experimental and brain-imaging studies that I sampled in Chapters 2 and 3 have given us a fascinating snapshot of the mind of the psychopath. There is ample evidence that psychopaths see the world around them differently from the rest of us. Studies, like the ones that I covered in those chapters, can help illuminate what either motivates or fails to curb psychopathic behaviour. Individuals with psychopathy lack empathy, and are very focused on their own needs. They make poor and impulsive decisions, without properly computing the consequences of their actions. They also do not appear to derive the same enjoyment from affiliating with other people that the rest of us do. Unsurprisingly their brains are different too, as we would expect from people who feel and choose differently. But how did these individuals' brains get to be this way? What are the developmental origins of the psychopathic mind? Is psychopathy a genetic condition, or do people become psychopaths because they have been maltreated? Is it inevitable that someone who displays psychopathic features in childhood will become an adult psychopath?

In this chapter I will outline what we know so far regarding the risk factors for psychopathy and how confident we can be of their causality. I will also consider how atypical feeling and thought processes may evolve over development. Research that is focused on answering these questions has increased exponentially in the past five to ten years alone, and although there is still much to be discovered, the data that are accumulating are providing helpful signposts for researchers and clinicians. There are also many interesting new avenues of research that scientists are pursuing in order to find out more.

Is psychopathy a genetic disorder?

We have robust evidence of genetic risk for psychopathic traits from twin studies. The twin method is a natural experiment that relies on the different levels of genetic relatedness between identical and fraternal twin pairs to estimate the contribution of genetic and environmental factors to individual differences in the population. In plain English, this means that we can use twins to study how much differences between those individuals who score extremely highly, in the middle, or at the low end of psychopathic traits are due to genetic or environmental factors. The specific genes or environments that account for differences in psychopathy between individuals are not identified in the twin analyses. Rather, they provide the sum total estimate of the degree to which genetic and environmental influences matter in explaining variation in the population. These estimates represent any and all genes or environments that explain why some individuals exhibit more psychopathic features than others.

The basic premise of the twin method is this: if identical twins, who share 100 per cent of their genetic material, appear more similar on a trait than fraternal twins, who share on average 50 per cent of their segregating genetic material (like any siblings), then we can infer that there are genetic influences on a trait. Identical twins' genetic similarity is twice that of fraternal twins'. If nothing apart from genes influences similarity in a behaviour/ trait, then we would expect the identical twins to be twice as similar with respect to psychopathic traits as fraternal twins (Figure 10a).

Shared environmental influences—ones that make family members (including twins) similar to each other—are inferred if fraternal twins are more similar to each other than you would expect purely on the basis of them sharing 50 per cent of their genetic material (i.e. if their resemblance is very similar to identical twin resemblance, rather than half of it—which is what would be expected if only genes were important for similarity among family members) (Figure 10b).

Finally, if identical twins are not 100 per cent similar on a trait (as would be expected if only genes influenced a trait), non-shared environmental influences are inferred—in other words, environmental influences that make twins different from each other (Figure 10c). The non-shared environmental estimate also includes measurement error.

All approaches to studying human character and behaviour have some inherent limitations, as we (thankfully) cannot manipulate

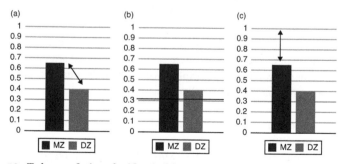

10. Twin correlations for identical (monozygotic; MZ) and fraternal (dizygotic; DZ) twins. MZ twins resemble each other more than DZ twins, indicating genetic influences on a trait (a). If DZ twin similarity is greater than you would expect purely on the basis of them sharing 50 per cent of their genetic material, this indicates the importance of shared environmental factors on a trait (b). Finally, if identical twins are not 100 per cent similar on a trait (as would be expected if only genes influenced a trait), non-shared, individual specific environmental influences are inferred (c).

risk and protective factors at will. Scientists have to rely on a number of different methods to gain confidence that their findings are real, rather than a fluke. One might argue that findings from twin studies are biased because people are inclined to exaggerate identical twins' similarity to each other (interestingly, studies show that identical twins who live apart are also rated very similarly on a number of psychological traits, although those who rate them cannot compare the two twins). Importantly, adoption studies corroborate the findings from twin studies and also indicate that there is a genetic risk for psychopathic traits (the same is true for a number of other psychological traits).

It is always reassuring when different research designs converge on similar findings. When children are adopted away, they grow up with parents (and often siblings) who are not genetically related to them. This enables scientists to study pairs of individuals who either share some genes, but do not share their home environment (e.g. biological parent and their child who has been adopted away)—or conversely share their home environment, but are not each other's biological relatives and therefore do not share more genes than random strangers who meet on the street (e.g. adoptive parent and their adopted child). If there is an association between the biological parent's psychopathic traits and their adopted away child's psychopathic traits (although the child has been adopted away shortly after birth and has not been parented by their biological parent), then this is evidence of genetic risk for psychopathy. An association between an adoptive parent's parenting style and the adopted child's psychopathic traits would provide strong evidence for environmental influences on risk for psychopathy.

Twin and adoption studies have demonstrated that psychopathic personality traits are moderately to strongly heritable in children and adults. Research I have conducted together with Professor Robert Plomin from King's College London suggests that psychopathic antisocial behaviour may be more heritable than antisocial behaviour that is not accompanied by psychopathic features. In short, genetic differences between individuals can explain why some individuals are at an increased risk of developing psychopathic personality features and the antisocial behaviour that often co-occurs with these features.

When studying any heritability figures for a complex behavioural phenotype like psychopathy, it is very important to remember that a moderate to strong heritability does not mean that someone is destined to become a psychopath. There is always a degree of error in these estimates (they are not precise) and the relative importance of genetic influences may differ between populations (to illustrate, if adequate nutrition is available, individual differences in height in the population are almost exclusively explained by genetic differences between individuals; if parts of the population suffer from malnutrition, then individual differences in height will in part be explained by environmental factors, namely availability of nutrition). Most critically, the heritability estimates do not tell us anything about the origins of psychopathic features for a specific, single individual or the extent to which that individual's presentation is due to their genetic make-up.

I would also like to point out that there are no genes for psychopathy. This may sound like a bizarre claim, as I have just said that data (including data from my own research) clearly show that psychopathic traits are heritable, but let me explain. The way that genetic risk for psychopathy operates is likely to be probabilistic, rather than deterministic: genes do not directly code for psychopathy. But genes do code for proteins that influence characteristics such as neurocognitive vulnerabilities that may in turn increase the risk for developing psychopathy, particularly under certain environmental conditions.

Psychopathy is not a single gene disorder, unlike, for example, Huntington's. Individuals who suffer from Huntington's have a faulty copy of a gene that will definitely cause this devastating disorder. The faulty gene results in the death of brain cells and eventually in the death of the person who carries the gene. In cases like Huntington's, when the gene is found, scientists have a clear target and a set of biological processes that they can focus on. Thankfully drugs are being trialled for treatment of Huntington's that lower the level of the harmful huntingtin protein in the nervous system.

Genes that are implicated as risk genes for psychopathy are likely to include genes that confer advantages, as well as disadvantages, depending on the full set of other genes that an individual has, as well as the individual's environmental context (more of the environment soon). Although a person's genome (in other words their whole set of genes) likely limits the 'range for phenotypic expression', it does not pre-specify how an individual will turn out. The specific developmental trajectory of any individual is determined by a complex interplay between genetic propensities and environmental factors that constrain how those genetic propensities are expressed across development. This is why we need to get better at studying development when we want to understand how disorders such as psychopathy come about and how we might prevent them.

Twin and adoption studies only tell us about the relative importance of genetic influences in explaining variation in the degree of psychopathic traits that different individuals exhibit. These studies do not identify the specific risk genes that are involved. Because the brains, information processing, and some behaviours associated with psychopathy are at least partially distinct from those associated with antisocial behaviour in general, researchers think that the risk genes for psychopathy may not always be the same as risk genes for antisocial behaviour in the absence of psychopathic traits. We can make reasonable guesses regarding the risk genes—for example, those genes that have an impact on the range of emotional reactivity, empathy, and capacity for attachment are likely to be important. The problem is, most of these genes are yet to be found. Not just in relation to psychopathy, but in general.

Only a handful of molecular genetic investigations have focused on psychopathic traits and have identified particular serotonin and oxytocin system genes—thought to contribute to emotional reactivity and capacity for attachment—as increasing risk of psychopathy. Such findings are exciting, but they need to be replicated in larger samples to evaluate whether they represent robust associations. In addition to candidate gene studies that focus on just one genotype, Professor Robert Plomin and I have collaborated on conducting genome-wide association studies on risk of developing psychopathy. The genome-wide association studies do not just focus on a single or few candidate genes, but instead comb across the genome for common genetic variation that may be associated with psychopathic traits. Disappointingly, our studies have not unearthed any genetic variants with a large effect on risk of developing psychopathy—but this has been the story of most psychiatric phenotypes.

Why has it been so difficult to find the genes that increase the risk of developing psychopathy when the twin and adoption studies indicate that psychopathy has a substantial heritable component? There are several reasons. Molecular genetic research into other heritable conditions, such as autism and schizophrenia, is a lot more advanced than genetic research into psychopathy. Big international scientific consortiums have worked on large samples and rich clinical data to look for genes associated with these two serious conditions. Such large-scale scientific efforts have shown us that genetic risk for most disorders, even those that are strongly heritable, is 'polygenic'. In other words, we are very unlikely to be searching for a few devastating genes that push certain individuals to a risk group. Instead we are hunting for multiple genes of small effect size that probabilistically increase the risk of developing the disorder. This of course makes our task of finding the genes a lot more difficult. Finding genes that have a small effect will require very large sample sizes and unfortunately molecular genetic studies of psychopathy have had small sample sizes to date. We have not yet had large international scientific consortia focus on the genetic underpinnings of psychopathy, and many large-scale studies do not include good measures of psychopathic personality.

It is also very likely that we need to get better at understanding how genes interact with other genes, as well as environmental risk, if we want to get a better sense of how the genetic risk for psychopathy manifests across development. We may only see the effects of particular risk genes if they are combined with other risk genes or with environmental risk factors that are necessary for the effects of those genes to play out.

Exciting new methodological developments give hope that the progress in gene hunting will continue apace. Genetic research is likely to advance greatly in the coming decade, including studies that focus on finding rare genetic variants that may have a large effect on risk for psychopathy, but may only affect a small subset of population. Molecular genetic studies of psychopathy have not, so far, looked for rare variants, but this approach has unearthed some interesting findings in other areas of psychiatric genetics, including autism and schizophrenia research.

There is also a strong interest in using novel epigenetic approaches that may help uncover mechanisms of gene–environment interaction in increasing psychopathy risk. Epigenetics refers to changes in gene expression (i.e. in how much of the protein that the gene produces is expressed). Some of these epigenetic changes in gene expression are heritable (i.e. due to the individual's genetic predisposition), but both animal and human data indicate that environmental factors (such as extreme stress) can also alter gene expression. The underlying DNA remains the same, but the gene activity can differ. There is tentative evidence of epigenetic changes involving the oxytocin receptor gene at birth, and subsequent risk of developing psychopathic traits in adolescence. At the moment we do not know if these epigenetic changes reflect genetic or environmental risk factors in those with psychopathic traits.

Is psychopathy the result of environmental adversity?

Both cross-sectional and longitudinal studies identify maltreatment, harsh discipline, negative parental emotions, and disorganized attachment with the caregiver as risk factors associated with antisocial behaviour and psychopathic features. In contrast, warm and consistent parenting has been associated with reduced risk of antisocial behaviour and psychopathy.

Examining data from these studies, as well as reading and hearing media reports about the backgrounds of people who commit crimes, can lead us to reasonably assume that 'bad parenting' or maltreatment causes antisocial behaviour and psychopathy. Yet we need to examine such reports and our own assumptions with caution. An age-old adage in research is that 'correlation is not causation'. We may see a relationship between two variables (e.g. harsh parenting and psychopathy), but we cannot jump to a simple conclusion that 'harsh parenting causes psychopathy' from observing this association.

The first qualifier that we need to be mindful of is that not everybody who experiences maltreatment, harsh parenting, or less than optimal attachment with their caregivers develops psychopathy as they grow up. The majority do not. Furthermore, many individuals with psychopathy have not experienced maltreatment or harsh parenting when they were growing up. This indicates that these risk factors are neither necessary, nor sufficient to bring about this disorder (and neither are genes—let's not forget that!). The quality of parenting clearly matters for children—I am absolutely not arguing that it does not—but the precise way in which parenting shapes the child's development is complex. Not every child reacts to a particular environment in the same way, even when that environment is very atypical and adverse. It is also important to note that different children have different needs and present different challenges to their caregivers.

This brings me to another important qualifier, one that we are less used to thinking about. Several risk factors that are commonly thought to be 'environmental' may in part reflect the genetic predispositions of people who are part of that environment—a phenomenon known as *gene–environment correlation*. Children, as well as the adults who interact with them, have substantial, in part heritable, individual differences in their social information-processing capacities and behaviour. Not all children are equally cooperative, empathetic, loving, or easy to manage. And not all adults are equally responsive to social cues, or able to regulate their emotions or plan ahead. Individual differences in a variety of social-cognitive abilities clearly impact how children behave and what they best respond to, as well as how adults behave and how they respond to the child or meet his/her needs. Just as we are not going to find one gene that will explain why someone becomes a psychopath, it is also helpful to assume that 'it's complicated' when we seek to understand environmental risk.

In typical families where family members are biologically related to each other, the parents and children share genetic endowments and information-processing styles. This is likely to constrain the range of 'inputs' and learning outcomes that are probable for a particular child and may explain why behaviours develop in certain ways in particular family ecologies. Parents with genetic risk factors for psychopathy and antisocial behaviour are likely to display parenting behaviours in line with these risks (e.g. harsh and inconsistent parenting or difficulty in relating to the emotions of their children). They may also pass on some of their risk genes to their offspring, which can increase the chance of the child developing disruptive behaviours and lack of empathy. This means that part of the association between less harsh parenting and psychopathic traits in the child may represent a genetic confound. Put differently, we cannot assume pure environmental causality when the association may in part be due to shared genetic risk between parents and offspring and may not entirely reflect a pure impact of parenting on child behaviour. Researchers call this type of genetic confound 'passive gene–environment correlation'.

We also know that some of the differences in the reactions that different children evoke in their caregivers are in part driven by heritable dispositions. Children at risk of developing psychopathy are extremely challenging to parent. They typically show diminished empathy for others, less remorse, tend to manipulate others, engage in self-serving behaviours, are impulsive, and show little interest in being nice to other people. It is not difficult to imagine how such children might be very difficult to parent. It is therefore likely that they evoke different parental feelings and behaviours than less challenging children and research suggests that this is indeed the case. This is another example of a potential genetic confound, something that researchers call *evocative gene–environment correlation.*

Children and adolescents also make specific choices that are not random, but instead are in line with their heritable dispositions. These can end up limiting the range of experiences that they have. This type of genetic confound is called *active gene–environment correlation.* For example, a child with a genetic predisposition to psychopathic traits might seek out delinquent gangs where they can manipulate sidekicks to help them deal drugs or rob people.

Without genetically informative longitudinal studies it is not possible to tell to what extent an association between e.g. harsh parenting and psychopathic features (or quality of attachment and psychopathic features) purely reflects environmental risk.

Environment is not just something that 'happens to us'. Individuals create, select, and modify their own environment. We are co-creators of our social ecologies. This has implications for understanding the development of psychopathy, as well as for designing interventions for the condition. Without accounting for gene–environment correlation, we cannot be sure as to how 'environmental risk' operates or the degree to which measures of parenting reflect genetic confounding.

Luckily we are starting to gather new data from longitudinal twin and adoption studies that have investigated parenting and the development of psychopathic traits, and are able to provide some control for the genetic confounds. Few twin studies, including one from my own group, have focused on identical twins who have received different treatment by their parents (e.g. more or less harsh or warm parenting). Because identical twins are each other's genetic clones, any difference in psychopathic traits that is related to difference in parenting can be said to reflect environmental causation. Findings from these twin studies are currently mixed and suggest that association between parenting and development of psychopathic traits can reflect environmental causation, but may also partly be due to shared genetic risk among parents and children (i.e. those parents who pass on risk genes for development of psychopathy are also less able to parent well).

Very encouraging adoption study data by Dr Luke Hyde's group from the University of Michigan has demonstrated that warm parenting by an adoptive mother is able to buffer the genetic risk for developing psychopathic traits. Children who have experienced this kind of adoptive parenting develop less psychopathic features than their adopted-away peers who also have a biological risk for antisocial behaviour and psychopathy (as indexed by the biological mother's disposition), but whose adoptive mothers are not able to provide consistent warm parenting. This study unequivocally demonstrated positive parenting can have a causal influence in reducing developmental risk for psychopathy.

It is tempting to conclude from the adoption data that if we just had parenting interventions that curb harsh parenting and promote warm parent–child interactions, then we could stop the development of psychopathy. It may not be quite so straightforward as this, and the phenomenon of gene–environment correlation is also likely to explain why. Parents in adoptive families are typically very motivated to undertake the challenges of parenting, are often relatively well resourced, and do not, as a rule, share the same constitutional vulnerabilities as the children they adopt. By contrast, in biological families, parents of children with psychopathic traits are more likely to have a host of genetic and contextual risk factors that are associated with life stress, and which can make it more difficult to deliver interventions that seek to promote consistent parenting and prosocial behaviour.

We also know that not all adoptive parents manage to parent the children with difficult temperaments in a way that promotes prosocial development. Some children are extremely difficult and evoke a host of negative feelings in their parents, no matter how motivated the parents are and how genuinely they want the best for their children. Some parents even describe parental 'burn out' in the face of repeated difficult interactions.

This point is illustrated in a chilling way in Lionel Shriver's book *We Need to Talk About Kevin*. This fictional account provides a believable portrait of a boy, Kevin, who goes on to commit a high-school massacre. Kevin's mother feels ambivalent about becoming a parent and struggles to connect with her son from the start. It would be all too easy to blame her for causing her son's deeply disturbing personality and behaviours. This is no doubt a mother who does not effortlessly take to parenting. Yet, anyone with a shred of empathy can see that it would be very hard, if not soul destroying, to parent someone like Kevin. He is impossible to soothe as a baby, he does not show love as a toddler, he is violent and unempathetic—animals and his sister are not safe. If everything was down to parenting a blank slate, one might expect

Kevin's sister to turn out like him, yet she does not. Kevin's mother may have her shortcomings, but she is not a bad mother and she does not have two disruptive children. Of course we are talking about fiction here, but I have talked to many parents over the years who identify with what is described in Shriver's book. They have tried their best, but their child is out of control.

Risk factors beyond parenting

A number of other factors, apart from parenting and parental attachment, may also contribute to the development of psychopathy. These include peer relationships, socio-economic status, and pre- and perinatal risk factors. Peer relationships of children at risk of developing psychopathy are characterized by instability and conflict. Such children also more frequently associate with delinquent friends, yet they seem to be the ringleaders. It appears to be their behaviour that influences their friends', not the other way around. Neighbourhoods with lower resources (lower socio-economic status) have also been observed to promote the development of psychopathic traits in individuals at genetic risk.

We need a lot more data to understand how environmental risk factors such as these operate and to what degree there is an element of genetic confounding. For example, children do not choose their friends at random and associations between delinquent peers and child psychopathic traits are bound to reflect genetic propensities for selecting particular friendship groups, as well as the impact of interacting with such friends over time. Growing up in low-resource neighbourhoods clearly does not turn most individuals into psychopaths, but it may be that psychopathic personality traits enable someone to ruthlessly exploit the scarce resources in such environments.

We know very little about pre- and perinatal environmental risk factors (e.g. maternal smoking during pregnancy, maternal psychopathology during pregnancy, and birth complications) and the development of psychopathy. One study to date has reported an association between maternal mental health problems during and after pregnancy and subsequent child psychopathic traits, but it is not clear whether this association is causal. It may also partly reflect family-level genetic vulnerability.

In this context, it is instructive to consider a recent, innovative study on maternal smoking and child antisocial behaviour led by Dr Frances Rice and Professor Anita Thapar at the University of Cardiff. Several large-scale epidemiological studies had shown that there is an association between maternal smoking during pregnancy and child antisocial behaviour. However, until very recently we did not know whether this association was causal. To examine this, Dr Rice and Professor Thapar collected data from children conceived with in vitro fertilization (IVF), whose mothers had either smoked or not smoked during pregnancy. The children were either genetically related to their mothers (IVF with the mother's own egg) or not genetically related to their mothers (IVF with a donor egg). This design enabled the scientists to show that maternal smoking was associated with child antisocial behaviour in only those mother–child pairs where the mother and child were related to each other. If the mother smoked, but the child was not genetically related to the mother (donor egg pairs), there was no association between smoking during pregnancy and subsequent child antisocial behaviour.

Of course Dr Rice and Professor Thapar did not argue that smoking is harmless for babies. Regardless of whether the mothers and babies were genetically related to each other or not, smoking had an impact on the birth weight of the baby. However, this study did suggest that perhaps temperamental factors that make it more likely for a mother to continue smoking during pregnancy also increase the child's risk of developing antisocial behaviour, while the smoking itself is not a causal risk factor for antisocial behaviour. We are yet to conduct similar studies with regard to psychopathy, but when we do, it will be important that researchers use study designs that permit evaluation of whether the pre- and perinatal risk factors play a truly causal role in the development of psychopathy.

The fact that most social environmental factors are likely to be 'confounded' by genetics does not mean that we should write off the environment. But it does mean that we should not be lazy and assume simple, straightforward causation between a proposed environmental risk factor and psychopathy. In fact, if we hope to prevent the development of psychopathy or treat psychopathic features when they are already accompanied by problematic behaviours, we need to understand what risk factors are causal and how they operate. This will help us tailor interventions that are focused on the needs of particular individuals and families and help us not to waste effort and financial resources on interventions that do not work.

In this context it is also important to briefly consider that there may be some individuals who develop what look like psychopathic (callous, unemotional, self-serving) behaviours, but who do not have the characteristic profile of lack of fear and emotional underarousal to other people's distress. These individuals are often termed 'secondary psychopaths' by researchers. I prefer to say that they present with a 'behavioural phenocopy'.

Phenocopy is a term that refers to a presentation that is similar on the surface, but has different underlying causes. I have used this term loosely to refer to my assumption that these are individuals who present with psychopathic features and behaviours, but who do not have the genetic or neurocognitive risk profile of 'classic', 'primary psychopaths'. They display behaviours that look uncaring, unempathetic, and cold, but when you scratch the surface, differences emerge. Dr Eva Kimonis from the University of New South Wales has done important research showing that childhood maltreatment can at times lead to a behavioural presentation that looks callous, but with an underlying profile of extreme emotional reactivity that looks very different to that which we typically associate with psychopathy. I will not discuss these individuals further as this *Very Short Introduction* is focused on 'classic' psychopathy. However, it is important to know that this group exists, and they serve as a reminder that there may be different pathways to psychopathic behaviour.

How can we best understand the development of psychopathy?

It is very tiresome to see how much mileage can still be gained from the red herring that is 'the nature vs. nurture debate'. That debate is long dead and should be buried. If we want to understand how atypical cognitions—such as inability to resonate with others' distress or find affiliative signals rewarding—arise in psychopathy, we need to understand the complex interplay between genetic and environmental constraints in shaping brain development. It is my frustrating experience that the minute you report findings from a brain-imaging study, such as those discussed in the previous chapters, the press are prone to assume that you are claiming that something is biologically hard-wired and immutable. This is why I tend to put out any press release of our research with a considerable 'health warning'. The brain is a learning organ. The primary purpose of the brain is to help us navigate our environment by learning about it. Individuals vary in their genetic endowments and consequently in their readiness to learn about particular environmental contingencies. The brain also shapes the environment and social ecology around the individual via behaviours it effects and via its interpretation and prediction of the world. In other words, no one is born a 'tabula rasa', a blank slate—we are all born with some constraints that shape our learning and the learning environment. And the environment also in turn shapes the brain. We should not ask whether a disorder is biological or environmental, we should seek to understand a disorder as a developmental progression of a particular hand of endowments—genetic and environmental—dealt to an individual.

Sadly we currently lack longitudinal data that chart the development of 'psychopathic cognitions' in a way that would enable us to understand gene–environment interplay in an intricate manner. But we can piece together data from different studies and make educated hypotheses of what might happen over development. Speculation like this is something that tends to make scientists, myself included, mildly uncomfortable. But as long as we keep in mind that we are putting forward hypotheses that should be tested, not data, this exercise can help us illustrate what we are likely up against when we try to understand how a disorder like psychopathy arises. Can we make reasonable predictions regarding how, for example, lack of empathy or reduced drive to affiliate come about? What sorts of processes would we want to investigate over development to understand how a juvenile with psychopathic features or an adult criminal psychopath presents?

What could drive atypical development of empathy in psychopathy?

We have rich data robustly showing us that psychopaths behave in ways that show profound lack of empathy and concern for others' welfare. Experimental findings from incarcerated adults, children at risk of developing psychopathy, and community samples suggest that individuals with high levels of psychopathic traits do not readily identify other people's distress, are not distracted by it, do not resonate with it, and do not experience guilt. We also have ample data from brain-imaging studies showing us that those brain networks that support resonating with other people's distress, empathizing with them, feeling guilt, and so forth are not functioning typically in individuals with high levels of psychopathic traits. What might be at the root of the psychopath's difficulty in recognizing other people's emotions and empathizing with them?

One possibility is that because they have genetic propensities predisposing to lower arousal and reactivity, individuals with psychopathy have less strong emotional reactions to situations that typically generate distress in other people. Over time, as a baby with this profile develops through childhood, the less strong emotional reactivity may lead to a reduced ability to process and recognize distress cues in other people. Emotional contagion, which is necessary for empathy to occur, develops through the repeated pairing of a person's own emotional state with cues denoting the same state in another (the other person's expressions, postures, vocalizations).

Mothers typically mimic ('mirror back') their infants' emotional expressions when they observe the infant experiencing an emotion. If the infant experiences distress less often than is typical, there will be reduced opportunity for the infant to learn which cues reliably signal distress as their mothers will have fewer opportunities to mirror emotions back to them. Recent data from Professor Mark Dadds's group at the University of Sydney suggest that children at risk of developing psychopathy do not seek out eye contact with their mothers (although the mothers themselves do not differ from mothers of typically developing children in seeking out eye contact with their children). It is unclear what underlies this reduced drive to seek eye contact, but as these children grow up this is likely to further restrict learning opportunities about emotions for them.

In other words, over time children at risk of developing psychopathy are likely to form relatively impoverished representations of their own emotions (and there is some evidence for this), which in turn makes it more difficult for them to reliably identify and empathize with other people's emotional experience.

They cannot effectively 'anchor' other people's displays of distress to a robust representation of the same state in themselves.

Why don't individuals with psychopathy develop normal social relationships?

As we have seen in the previous chapter, a particular hallmark of individuals with psychopathy is their reduced motivation and capacity to develop social relationships founded on an enjoyment of prosocial interaction or genuine love and concern for others' well-being. The reasons for this presentation have received less empirical attention than lack of empathy. New data suggest that those cognitive and neural processes that make social stimuli rewarding and support feelings of affiliation and cohesion may be atypical in individuals with high levels of psychopathic features. Such stimuli do not seem to have the same motivational value for them, and other people's emotions, thoughts, and needs are not automatically attended to or prioritized. But why is this the case?

We know from animal work that dopamine orients individuals to primary rewards like food and sex, while orienting to social reward (e.g. other members of the same species, including the primary caregiver) depends on the co-activation of the dopamine and oxytocin systems. Oxytocin is involved in tuning the levels of arousal that individuals experience during social interactions. It also promotes focus towards social stimuli (something that seems to be atypical in children who have or go on to develop psychopathic features). When oxytocin release happens together with dopamine ('the pleasure hormone') release, the important social interactions are coded as rewarding in the brain. This in turn helps maintain focus to socially relevant stimuli and promotes so-called 'biobehavioural synchrony' between the child and the caregiver over development. Biobehavioural synchrony refers to the ability of the parent and the child to coordinate mutual interaction.

The development of brain networks that support affiliative and attachment behaviours, such as biobehavioural synchrony, happens in response to dopamine and oxytocin inputs over time. If an individual reliably experiences arousal that causes them to focus on other people (first the caregiver, then a wider set of people), and if this focus is accompanied by the release of dopamine and feelings of pleasure, this sets up the fundamental building blocks for developing social affiliation.

It is not unreasonable to hypothesize that infants who are at genetic risk of developing psychopathy are more vulnerable to atypical early development of biobehavioural synchrony. A few studies implicate genetic variants which predispose to reduced functioning of the oxytocin system in the development of psychopathy. There is also tentative evidence that there may be disruption of biobehavioural synchrony, driven by the child, or both the child and the parent (a 'double hazard'), in infants at risk of developing psychopathic features. Those who either have or go on to develop psychopathic traits in childhood seek out less eye contact with their mothers as infants and children. We can speculate that atypical biobehavioural synchrony may have a knock-on effect for development, where brain circuits responsible for initiating and maintaining affiliation/attachment are not calibrated in a typical way in individuals who go on to develop psychopathy. This may mean that the child misses displays of positive emotion and will not code interactions with others as socially rewarding. It may also impact the child's tendency to spontaneously consider other minds.

What do we still need to know?

We desperately need more longitudinal data that combine a number of different methods to study the development of psychopathy. We know that not everyone with psychopathic features in childhood goes on to develop adult psychopathy. What are the key ingredients for risk and remission? I look forward to a future date when we have a better understanding of the genes that increase the risk of developing psychopathy. If, for example, we were able to identify a set of risk genes that relate to the functioning of systems important for supporting the development of social affiliation (e.g. oxytocin release and regulation), these could be used in longitudinal samples followed up from infancy. This would enable scientists to test, for example, whether infants with high polygenic risk scores (e.g. a large number of risk genes) have significant disruptions to the early development of biobehavioural synchrony—which the scientists can measure by using standard tasks of face orienting and gaze following. Such studies would enable scientists to ask targeted questions about gene–environment interplay and how it unfolds.

We might also ask whether infants at genetic risk shape parental responses and impact the formation of biobehavioural synchrony in a different way from their peers with low genetic risk? Researchers could also investigate whether particular parenting behaviours or other environmental factors exacerbate elevated genetic risk for disrupted biobehavioural synchrony. What would be the knock-on effects of atypical social reward processing and diminished capacity to spontaneously consider other minds? Many of these questions could be most conclusively addressed in the context of infants who have been adopted away at birth, as in this case the researchers could be confident that they are measuring the impact of environment on top of genetic risk, rather than passive gene–environment correlation. Although there is so much that we still need to find out, the extant findings are already helpful when we think about interventions. This is what I want to consider next.

Chapter 5
What to do with a psychopath?

Not only are there substantial costs associated with psychopathy for society, but individuals with psychopathy often cause devastating emotional, financial, and physical damage to their victims. They can be physically, emotionally, and sexually abusive to their partners or scam work colleagues out of their life savings. The existence of organizations such as the Aftermath Foundation for Surviving Psychopathy, dedicated to providing information and support for victims of psychopaths, is a testament to the havoc these individuals wreak in other people's lives.

People are naturally keen to know whether it is possible to treat or prevent psychopathy. Research findings can guide our expectations regarding what should work and how the current intervention approaches might be tailored to be more effective for individuals with or at risk of developing psychopathy. There has also been substantial interest in whether genetic, brain-imaging, and environmental risk factor findings should have a bearing on sentencing decisions for individuals with psychopathy, a topic that is ripe for provocative headlines in the tabloid press. I hope that having read the previous chapters, the reader will already be sceptical regarding the usefulness of current data for individual sentencing decisions—if not, I will do my very best to promote healthy scepticism. I also want to promote optimism. Systematic research will help us build a better evidence base, which will assist us in making more informed policy, clinical and sentencing decisions.

Can adults with psychopathy be treated?

There is received wisdom that psychopathy is untreatable, and this belief seems relatively unshakeable among many clinicians, researchers, and lay people. Certainly there are studies that seem to suggest that various therapies—including psychoanalysis, group therapy, or drug treatments—all make very little difference to the behaviour of psychopaths or their ability to feel for other people. There have also been reports that individuals with psychopathy may even use techniques that they have picked up in therapeutic programmes to manipulate their future victims with increased efficiency. In Robert Hare's seminal book *Without Conscience*, he tells of an inmate who described therapy in the following way: 'These programmes are like a finishing school. They teach you how to put the squeeze on people.'

Individuals with psychopathy are four to eight times more likely to reoffend after release than non-psychopathic inmates. We know from the broader literature on antisocial behaviour and criminality that those individuals who persist with their antisocial behaviour increasingly diverge from their peers over development. They do not usually achieve the same educational, employment, and relationship milestones as other people and this means that as time passes, it will be ever more challenging for them to integrate back into society.

Let us imagine an adult psychopath with a long criminal history. He has led a number of illegal operations that have helped him accumulate money and gain kudos among his criminal peers and the opposite sex. He has had multiple sexual partners before incarceration and is generally used to 'running the show'. And he most certainly does not feel bad or guilty about his behaviour, he is just cross that he got caught and feels that the only injustice in the whole equation is that he has to spend time in prison. Most therapies depend on an individual feeling that they have problems and rely on their willingness to work under someone's direction to solve those problems. Sadly, individuals with psychopathy do not tend to feel like they have a problem or need help. They also do not like to submit to someone else's guidance. It is not difficult to see that a person with a history and disposition (including a grandiose sense of self-worth) that I just described might not feel motivated to engage in therapy in order to lead a non-criminal life—especially if such a life does not promise financial solvency or status. Does this mean that we should be wholly pessimistic about individuals with psychopathy, that there is no hope of behaviour change?

Before we throw in the towel altogether, we should consider several things. First, a number of individuals with psychopathy stop offending or reduce offending behaviour, even in the absence of therapeutic interventions (and I am not just talking here about those individuals who are incarcerated in institutions where they are unable to carry on offending). This becomes more common as individuals with psychopathy age. It has been speculated that, in some cases, this phenomenon relates to reduced scope for physical aggression as offenders grow older and become more frail. If you are not as strong as you used to be, you will not be able to readily engage in violent intimidation—should that have been an important part of your repertoire. It is also possible that educational programmes offered in some prison regimes help some individuals with psychopathy, perhaps those who are more cognitively able. Such programmes can enable offenders to plan ahead and regulate their behaviour and help them gain academic or vocational qualifications—all of which makes accumulating material rewards via legal means more possible.

Second, most of the studies on psychopathy and responsiveness to treatment have not been conducted in a way that meets current scientific and methodological standards. It would therefore be premature to make strong conclusions about the treatability of psychopathy based on those studies. Many of the existing studies have not had appropriate comparison data (e.g. from individuals on treatment waiting lists or receiving a different kind of treatment). It is also lamentable that many treatment studies have involved interventions that only last for a short duration or have reported outcomes that can give rise to undue pessimism. If the treatment outcome is specified as an absence of a disorder, then individuals with serious and pervasive problems and a lifelong history of disruptive behaviours are very unlikely to magically metamorphose into asymptomatic citizens following a short therapeutic intervention. However, they may show some changes for the better, and current treatment studies aim to measure improvements more sensitively and have demonstrated that there is some cause for hope.

There is no doubt that individuals with a serious personality disorder like psychopathy are difficult to treat. No one would argue otherwise. These individuals have a prolonged history of extremely atypical behaviour and unusual social interactions. They can be very disruptive in therapeutic settings, and many therapeutic settings are not designed to deal with the kind of behaviour they exhibit. For example, someone who is manipulative and lacks empathy can derail group therapy interventions. In every way possible, individuals with psychopathy present a substantial challenge. Yet, as an optimist, I remain cautiously hopeful that it is possible to have a therapeutic impact with adult psychopaths, but achieving such an impact is likely to be very difficult.

This brings me to two further considerations that are important to weigh up when we think about interventions. We do not currently know to what extent it is possible to change particular psychopathic traits and cognitions, such as lack of empathy and concern for others. Is it perhaps more realistic to find another way of ensuring that individuals with psychopathy behave in ways that do not violate the rights of others, even if they cannot be made to feel true empathy? And, should we concentrate more effort on prevention and intervention work in childhood and adolescence?

Can you train empathy and concern for others?

In July 2013 the BBC published a science news story with a headline: 'Psychopathic criminals have empathy switch'. They were reporting on a finding from a Dutch neuroimaging study of adult psychopaths, which showed that the psychopaths were less likely to spontaneously engage brain regions that are usually involved when people empathize with others, but could engage the same brain areas when they were asked to actively concentrate on feeling for other people. This finding was heralded in the media as showing that psychopaths can empathize with other people and could potentially be trained in empathy, thus bringing hope for rehabilitation. This is certainly worth testing empirically, but I am among the scientists who remain cautious about whether such an approach will truly revolutionize the treatment of psychopathy.

It is important not to overinterpret brain activation findings. The brain areas that responded when psychopaths were asked to actively imagine the emotional state of other people are the brain areas that are involved in introspection about feeling states. Thus, the study was able to show that when asked to explicitly introspect about feelings, both individuals with psychopathy and control participants activate the brain area that is typically engaged in introspection. However, the brain activation findings are not able to precisely pinpoint the experience of the feelings during this exercise, or the degree to which individuals with psychopathy had a qualitatively similar experience of empathy to controls. One might surmise that without a developmental history of automatically, spontaneously resonating with other people's feelings, the empathetic experience of individuals with psychopathy would be quite different from that of the controls', even when both are engaged in introspection and activate the same brain areas when doing so.

Even if we accepted the premise that individuals with psychopathy can be made to feel for others in the same way as controls do, does this mean that they would reliably do so after a period of effortful training? And are we confident that they would be motivated and committed to engage in such a training activity? A striking feature of empathetic response is that it is spontaneous, not something that most people have to concentrate on producing. We often feel distressed as a result of empathizing with other people who are in distress. This is not usually a nice thing to feel, but we cannot help it, it was not something that we chose or 'dialled up'. Research from different research groups shows that in order for people to engage in prosocial, helping behaviours towards those who appear to be in distress, they need to regulate their own emotions, the distress they feel because they have spontaneously empathized with someone.

In other words, being empathetic and behaving empathetically is not necessarily a pleasant experience, but instead involves having to experience and regulate a lot of negative arousal. If you do not spontaneously experience this negative arousal, what would motivate you to seek it out? Particularly if you feel reasonably comfortable with your existence and view your unemotional response to other people as an asset, as many psychopaths do. We might argue that evoking a spontaneous empathetic response (rather than an effortful one) in individuals with psychopathy should be our ultimate goal—but it is difficult for me to imagine how this could be achieved without some dubious, *Clockwork Orange*-esque conditioning approaches, which frankly would and should not pass an ethics review.

Regardless, I would be delighted if my pessimism is proven wrong and empathy training does indeed produce results. And it may be that it could hold promise in child and adolescent populations. This is an empirical question, and I look forward to data that can arbitrate whether the capacity for spontaneous empathizing can be boosted in children at risk of developing psychopathy, contributing to more adaptive behaviour in the long term.

I also proffer an educated guess that even if we manage to develop successful methods for training empathy in individuals with or at risk of developing psychopathy, we will never be able to make these people very empathetic or considerate of others. We all function within a range curtailed by our genetic propensities. Someone with a genetic propensity to average intelligence will not be the next leading physicist for NASA. They may do somewhat better than average with a lot of hard work, but they are very unlikely to become a principal investigator in a world-leading scientific facility. Despite my strongest wishes, I will never be an Olympic-standard swimmer—even if we magically shave off some decades and I practise every day. I simply lack the optimal physical proportions of the likes of Michael Phelps (and perhaps there is only one of him) that would have made that an obvious dream to pursue. An anxiety-prone person can learn to live with and manage their condition (and is highly motivated to do so as they typically feel rotten), but will sadly never experience the degree of consistent relaxation that is achieved by those individuals blessed with a sunny and carefree disposition.

I have somewhat laboured the point here, but I would propose that a psychopath who does not spontaneously resonate with other people's emotions is unlikely to become the most robust altruist around—even if we provide them with an intervention that produces some change in their propensity to empathize. Unlike individuals with anxiety, they lack a strong internal motivation to change how they feel—they are not the ones who feel rotten. This is why I do not think that empathy training alone will be sufficient to produce consistent prosocial behaviour in individuals with or at risk of developing psychopathy.

A serious and complex presentation such as psychopathy is likely to require multiple approaches. Knowing about the origins of psychopathy and the way that individuals with psychopathy think and feel is helpful when we try to think what might work to counter a full-blown disorder. We know that not only do individuals with psychopathy have difficulty in feeling empathy, they also suffer from a compromised ability to make good decisions, as they are poor at anticipating possible bad consequences to their actions, and do not always pay attention to the relevant information that would result in good decision making.

To make matters even more challenging, they do not seem to gain comparable pleasure from positive, affiliative emotions and interactions as their peers, and appear less motivated to please those around them. If typical socialization relies heavily on tools such as empathy induction (making children understand how their behaviour makes others feel), sanctions (punishing bad behaviour), and prosocial motivation (encouraging children to please others and belong), then those at risk of developing psychopathy can be viewed as having a blunted set of tools.

We can try to help them sharpen the tools, but we may also need to think of alternative means of socialization. Can we capitalize on their desire to 'look after number one' to promote prosocial behaviour, for example via material rewards? There are some very promising indicators that this may work, particularly for children and adolescents.

Do interventions work for children and adolescents at risk of developing psychopathy?

Unsurprisingly, there has been a lot of interest in interventions aimed at halting the development of psychopathy during childhood and adolescence. Interventions that are delivered earlier in life have the possibility of reaching an individual before they evolve entrenched patterns of antisocial behaviour and increasingly diverge from a typical path of development, and in the worst cases start committing crimes. I am often asked how early it is possible to reliably identify developmental risk for psychopathy and whether it would be best to intervene with very young children so that we might prevent psychopathic features from emerging in the first place. People are also rightly worried about labelling children unnecessarily and concerned about possible harm that could be caused by delivering interventions that might not, in fact, be needed.

Most Western governments run some universal programmes promoting healthy child development. These programmes are typically aimed at supporting parents and carers of infants and young children, from a variety of backgrounds, and provide material, health, psychological, and parenting support. Such programmes have been shown to reduce the long-term mental and physical health burden for the population—in other words, they show some effectiveness as a prevention tool. We lack good data on the impact of such programmes on the incidence of adult psychopathy, but it is perhaps safe to make a bet that they are, at the very least, unlikely to increase the rates of the disorder. They are also not likely to prevent all cases of psychopathy—even countries with very good universal programmes have criminal psychopaths.

From time to time you hear people suggest that it would be good if we could screen for psychopathy risk and target those children whom we worry about the most, before they develop serious symptoms. This sounds like a desirable goal, but it is not without complications. We are a long way off finding so-called 'biomarkers' (e.g. DNA or brain measures) that would help us pinpoint asymptomatic individuals at risk, and even if we had such tools it is unclear what their predictive power would be (more on this later in the chapter).

Early psychopathic traits are not an infallible prediction tool regarding who will develop adult psychopathy either. Data from our research group and others show that psychopathic traits and behaviours can decrease in some children, even without interventions. Would it be an appropriate use of resources to intervene with children whose problems might resolve themselves anyway? When is it appropriate to offer treatment for specific children and their families? I would argue that when a child or young person persistently behaves in a way that violates the rights of other people (by hurting them physically, emotionally, or materially), and when their behaviour limits their and other people's opportunities and safety—then there is a duty to intervene, for the sake of the child or young person and their family, but also for the sake of society more broadly. Even if their behaviour would resolve itself in the long run, the demonstrable harm to other people and the potential long-term harm for the child provide a strong imperative to act. What works in such circumstances? And what are the challenges in working with children at risk of developing psychopathy and their families?

There are a number of therapeutic approaches that have been developed to reduce antisocial behaviour in children and young people. When younger children present with behavioural problems, parents may be offered a place in a parenting programme that focuses on establishing good behaviour and encouraging more positive parent–child interactions. Such programmes can help the parent to more consistently reward their child's good behaviour. There is reasonable evidence to date that these programmes reduce levels of antisocial behaviour and increase prosocial behaviours in most children with behavioural problems, including those at risk of developing psychopathy.

With older children and young people, the interventions can involve individual or group therapy, or more broad-based approaches that consist of several different components. These components may focus on parent–child interactions, tools that help the child or young person manage their own behaviour, and can also involve schools, peers, and other entities that support the child or young person and their family. Such broad-based approaches may include different adults all adopting a similar approach to rewarding the child's or young person's good behaviour, monitoring the child's or young person's whereabouts, and communicating with each other. The child or young person may additionally have individual sessions with a therapist who can, for example, help them develop decision-making skills.

Broad-based programmes are also offered in some youth-offending institutions and often involve material rewards for good behaviour, individual therapy sessions, education, and leisure activities. There is some evidence that individual and broad-based approaches, in both community and young offender institutions, can reduce antisocial behaviour and psychopathic features in older children and young people, but we are less sure about which precise elements of these programmes work and why.

Parents, clinicians, and teachers are also acutely mindful of the fact that even when interventions have an impact, children and young people at risk of developing psychopathy have such severe levels of antisocial behaviour that they are often not ready for integration into mainstream society post-intervention. Although these children can show a degree of improvement that is comparable to their peers, they start the interventions with more problems and also finish with more problems.

What should researchers, practitioners, parents, and policymakers consider as they try to improve interventions for children at risk of developing psychopathy? This is something that I regularly think about with my colleague Professor Eamon McCrory, who co-directs the research unit at UCL with me. Eamon is a consultant clinical psychologist with extensive experience of working with children who display antisocial and psychopathic features. His insight has been critical for formulating ideas regarding the implications of our basic science findings for practice.

First, we may need longer and more intensive interventions for these children. If we take it as given that they start off with particularly severe and persistent behavioural problems, then we may want to offer them a larger quantity of therapy sessions and we may also want to introduce additional components to the therapy. These could include enhanced support to the parents and teachers, for example extensive help in delivering regular and consistent rewards for any hint of prosocial behaviour. Children at risk of developing psychopathy may also need different interventions at different stages of life. We do not know whether parenting intervention early in life will suffice, or whether the most vulnerable children will need additional interventions at subsequent stages of their life, such as individual sessions that focus on improving decision-making ability.

Unfortunately, provision for children who display a risk of developing psychopathy is not reliably, unequivocally good anywhere in the world. I find this situation both baffling and upsetting. We are failing these children and their families. It is near impossible to guarantee a referral to appropriate treatment. I have lost count of the desperate emails and phone calls that I receive from parents who want to do something, but who are simply unable to get the help and support that they need. I liken their situation to being told that: 'Yes, your child has a cancer, but we will wait to see if it metastasizes and at that point we will most likely not offer them cancer treatment, but will instead lock them up.' The sad thing is that ultimately we are not just failing the children at risk of developing psychopathy and their families, we are also failing society when we do not ensure that there are resources available for intervention. The financial and emotional costs of full-blown psychopathy are devastating and substantially outweigh any spending on early intervention. Sadly, the cost savings are not realized within the lifetime of a single government.

Second, we know that although most interventions, such as those focusing on parenting strategies, show effects at the group level, not every child benefits. We also know that it is extremely difficult to engage some children and their families in interventions. To optimize existing interventions, it is important to consider the phenomenon of gene–environment correlation, as well as what we know about the brains and thought processes of children at risk of developing psychopathy.

Interventions for children who display antisocial behaviour, including those at risk of developing psychopathy, predominantly draw on so-called systemic principles, focusing on the relationship between the child, their peers, and the adults around them (e.g. parents, carers, teachers, social workers). Yet, many aspects of establishing a mutual and balanced reciprocal relationship are contingent on emotional, prosocial, and affiliative processes that function quite differently in these children, as we have seen.

We need to systematically investigate whether we can develop alternative means of promoting prosocial behaviour, for example by helping the children see how they themselves benefit from being nice. We also need to develop a better understanding of the degree to which we can alter any aspects of information processing that are atypical, including those pertaining to the ability to empathize. In this context I would caution that we should not be fixated with normalizing empathy (even if we want to try that). From society's point of view, we just need people who are not dangerous and exploitative. It is also important to investigate whether there are sensitive developmental periods during which particular interventions are most effective.

Social learning principles used in therapeutic programmes emphasize the ways in which adult behaviour can impact on the child's or young person's outcome. The adults are urged to consistently reward good behaviour and ignore bad behaviour. This makes sense in theory, but can be very difficult to implement in practice. Children and young people also play a key role in shaping the responses of adults around them, they are active co-creators of their social environments, and in the case of those at risk of developing psychopathy, often evoke particularly negative reactions and a sense of parental inadequacy (or teacher incompetence). They furnish more infrequent occasions for parental (or teacher) praise or reward and behave in ways that are provocative and hard to ignore. This in turn increases the likelihood that the pattern of parent–child (or teacher–child) interaction becomes largely negative in tone. Furthermore, the biological parents of these children may themselves share some of the same vulnerabilities that characterize their child and may find it particularly hard to implement many aspects of typical parenting intervention programmes.

Helping parents, carers, and teachers reframe a child's behaviour in the context of a profile of different strengths and weaknesses may be helpful—it might not be possible to expect all the same things from these children as from their peers. Note, I am not arguing that these children should have a licence to violate the rights of other people. I am arguing that promoting adherence to social norms and moral codes might need to happen differently for them. Having systems in place to provide support for adults who interact with these children is likely to be critical. Most of us find parenting or teaching a typical child challenging enough. Parenting or teaching a child who does not show empathy, is nice only when they want something from you, hurts others, and is untrustworthy is difficult and can be soul destroying. Many parents and teachers feel burnt out. They are also, unsurprisingly, desperate for something that works, but have no idea what that something should be. Their usual parenting (or teaching) toolkit is not delivering. It is unreasonable to expect that most of us would be capable of intuitively parenting or teaching a child who responds so very differently from their siblings or peers. This challenge is magnified for those biological parents who share some of the same difficulties that their child has, for example in regulating their emotions, planning ahead, or being mindful of other people's emotions.

Most parents want what is best for their children, even if they have their own shortcomings (those who do not care or who intentionally harm their children are an exception). Intervention research and practice needs to focus on devising and evaluating ways of supporting healthy social development in children at risk of developing psychopathy, particularly when many of the building blocks that are typically used for this process come in different shapes to those available in the 'standard set'. The challenge may not only be in devising different strategies, but also in how 'palatable' such strategies feel to the adults. It is possible to promote prosocial behaviour by delivering constant rewards for good behaviour, ignoring bad behaviour, and appealing to someone's self-interest, yet it might take a saint to stick with this regime without active support—especially if the child is deliberately provocative, threatening, manipulative, and unkind. It can also offend adults' natural sense of fairness and moral correctness to ignore disruptive behaviour and help someone look after their self-interest, albeit prosocially.

Given the complex presentation of children at risk of developing psychopathy there is unlikely to be one easy silver bullet that will quickly normalize their behaviour. There are practical challenges in terms of the availability of sufficiently comprehensive and long-lasting interventions. There is also a need to develop a better understanding of possible alternative strategies for socialization that take into account the building blocks that are missing for children at risk. We also need means of supporting adults who have the difficult task of bringing up and educating these children. Gratifyingly this is an active area of research and colleagues in the UK, mainland Europe, Australia, and the US are devising and testing new approaches. There is great cause for optimism, particularly if governments deliver on their promises of promoting children's and young people's healthy development.

Should research findings have bearing on legal decision making?

Adults with psychopathy and young people at risk of developing the disorder do not only come to the attention of clinicians and educators, they are also likely to have a brush—or several—with the legal system. Should genetic risk and neural abnormalities bear on the sentencing decisions? Such questions are hotly debated among legal professionals, ethicists, moral philosophers, policymakers, and neuroscientists. The majority view is that the science is far from ready for the courtroom, but new findings come to light every day and today's conclusions may not be so self-evident tomorrow. Yet for now there remain difficulties in translating findings from the laboratory to bear on a case of a single individual within the legal setting.

All legal and policymaking changes must proceed with careful ethical consideration. The evidence based on genetic influences and neural correlates of psychopathy requires extension, refinement, and extensive replication before it can form the basis of legal recommendations. Current data suggest a degree of genetic vulnerability to the development of psychopathy, as well as several ways in which those with or at risk of developing psychopathy differ from typical individuals in how their brains process information. People have expressed worries about these scientific findings in two ways. Some are concerned that such findings can be used to argue for more lenient sentences for the carriers of risk genes or for those whose brains are 'different'. Others worry that they may result in prosecutors demanding harsher and longer (or 'preventative') sentences for the carriers of risk genes or those with atypical brain structure or function.

Are these concerns warranted? Astonishingly there is precedence from a handful of legal cases where either genetic or brain-imaging evidence has been used to argue for more lenient sentencing

decisions. For example, a court case in Italy admitted genotype evidence and this led to a reduced sentence for murder.
In contrast, a court case in the US used brain-imaging data to argue that an inmate could not be fully responsible for their behaviour and should be spared the death penalty. In this case, the evidence did not persuade the jury.

Science and law have different goals, and this means that the scientific findings do not always readily translate to legal settings. Genetic and brain-imaging studies of psychopathy are focused on explaining *individual differences* and *group differences, not* on explaining how a *single individual's offending* came about or what the odds are of them offending in the future. The legal system considers the probability of a given individual's guilt (or mitigating factors that might have a bearing on sentencing), as well as the likelihood that they might reoffend.

The current data firmly indicate that genetic vulnerability for psychopathy is not like genetic vulnerability for Huntington's disease (as discussed in Chapter 4). In the case of Huntington's a defect in a single gene is sufficient to cause the disease, and individuals who inherit the genetic mutation are certain to develop symptoms. Instead the genes involved in the risk for psychopathy act in a probabilistic manner and in concert with environmental factors to make some individuals more vulnerable to developing the condition. Findings from twin and adoption studies that report on the degree to which psychopathic features are heritable speak to variation in the population, not to a degree of individual risk. Alas, the information from these studies cannot be used to predict who will go on to develop psychopathy or the likelihood of someone reoffending.

But could or should such information be used as a mitigating factor in sentencing decisions in the future? Even if we were confident about the identity of the multiple genes that increase the risk of developing psychopathy, it is doubtful whether this knowledge would result in more mitigating pleas being made in the courtroom. The genes are not sufficient, on their own, to explain the person's psychopathic behaviour, and to the extent that they act in concert with environmental risk factors, litigators can already make mitigating pleas based on the known environmental risk circumstances. However, the knowledge that genes and environments interact could bolster the case for treating environmental risk as a mitigating factor. Litigators could argue that in someone with the defendant's genetic make-up, the environmental risk (such as childhood physical abuse or neglect) is even more likely to result in psychopathic behaviour than it would be in someone with a different genetic make-up. This is a hypothetical scenario in relation to psychopathy as we are very far away from identifying a set of risk genes for the condition that meet adequate scientific standards of proof.

In line with the genetic studies, brain-imaging studies look at the brain structure and function associated with group differences or individual differences in psychopathy; they do not provide diagnostic data on a single individual. Traumatic brain injury or brain tumours aside, we are not yet able to use individual brain scans as diagnostic tools. That has not stopped people from arguing that perhaps the neuroimaging findings should have a bearing on sentencing decisions. Should individuals with psychopathy be considered legally responsible if their brains do not generate appropriate emotional reactions that motivate moral behaviour? Or if they are unable to pay attention to the right things and consider the consequences of their actions?

Research conclusively shows that individuals with psychopathy are able to distinguish right from wrong, even if they do not 'feel it'. Being able to grasp this distinction forms a part of the current legal definitions regarding being of sound mind. However, the courts also consider whether an individual is capable of appreciating the nature and quality of their act, and here we might argue that those with psychopathy fare less well. Should we then not have compassion for them if they lack the essential ability for feeling that automatically hinders most of us from harming others? Surely they cannot be tried in the same way as those individuals who are capable of feeling empathy?

A congenitally blind individual cannot help that they are unable to see, yet we would not argue that they should be allowed to drive a car because being blind is not their fault. They would simply endanger too many people. We would hold a blind person accountable if they caused an accident while driving a car. When the inability to feel empathy is accompanied by a failure to behave in morally acceptable ways, the legal system must consider the right of the rest of society to be safe and not be exploited. I do not think that the current scientific findings provide a case for not holding individuals with psychopathy responsible for their crimes. I do, however, think that there is an argument for considering a treatment facility, rather than a prison, after sentencing and thus taking into account the evident handicap that individuals with psychopathy have (and I do not think we need genotypes of brain scans to diagnose that handicap). This could also prove to be a safer option for society. Treatment, rather than incarceration, is already applied in some countries, for example in the Netherlands.

The field is rapidly changing and new findings are accumulating daily. However, it is not yet possible to use information about a person's genetic or brain make-up to predict his or her risk of future behaviour or to definitively mitigate sentencing decisions. Whether such information should play a role in sentencing decisions in the future would depend on carefully conducted research demonstrating that such information can help prediction of risk over and above information gained by other well-established risk factors, such as prior offending history. It would also depend on policy decisions regarding whether a sentence should be served in a prison or at a treatment facility.

Things we need to know more about

All of the research I have discussed in this book is essentially concerned with trying to understand what makes individuals with psychopathy so different from the rest of us—how and why do they end up behaving the way they do? I proposed at the start of this book that part of our interest may relate to our fear of psychopaths. Could systematic research give us tools to help individuals at risk of developing psychopathy and their families, so that we might eventually have fewer psychopaths among us?

There is no doubt that our understanding of psychopathy has advanced substantially since Harvey Cleckley wrote *The Mask of Sanity* in the 1940s, Robert Hare developed the Psychopathy Checklist in the 1980s, and Paul Frick initiated the research into developmental risk for psychopathy in the 1990s. Even in the relatively short time that I have conducted research in the field, there has been a visible increase in the number of researchers studying psychopathy.

I attended the very first scientific meeting dedicated to psychopathy research in 2003, in Madison, Wisconsin. The meeting was convened by Professor Joe Newman, one of the scientists who has conducted seminal work into information-processing biases in psychopathy. I was a graduate student nearing the end of my PhD and hugely inspired by the exciting research presented by colleagues from the US, Canada, and Europe. It was a very small meeting. We all managed to fit into Joe's back garden for a barbecue at the end of the conference.

Since that first meeting the Society for Scientific Study of Psychopathy has been established and membership of the society has increased exponentially over the years. We now have many more research groups focusing on psychopathy than we did in

2003. New research is accumulating that focuses on genetics, brain structure, brain function, hormones, epigenetics, development, environmental risk, parenting, treatment—the list goes on. Yet there is so much we still do not know.

What are the genes that predispose to development of psychopathy? What is the role of epigenetics? How do genetic vulnerabilities shape social environments in ways that increase the risk of psychopathic presentation? Are there multiple developmental routes to psychopathy? (Probably.) How malleable are the brain processes associated with psychopathy? Are there particular periods when it is easier to change information-processing biases associated with a risk of developing psychopathy? I could go on.

What is eminently clear is that we need scientists and practitioners with different sets of expertise to work together to understand the development of psychopathy. To uncover how biological and social factors are intertwined over development in ways that result in such frightening presentation. A number of research groups are working on the outstanding research questions we still need to tackle. They are using new methods from epigenetics to computational psychiatry to improve classification of psychopathy and our understanding of how the condition develops.

The magnitude of what we do not yet know can seem daunting at times. Humans and their social ecologies are inherently complex. I am periodically jealous of scientific colleagues who manipulate matter at will on a petri dish. Or even those colleagues who work with animals and can perform careful controls of biological and social factors to study the development of behaviour. But the challenge of studying humans and our inherent curiosity about why we are all so different from one another is also what makes research into phenomena such as psychopathy so exciting and compelling.

References

Chapter 1: How can we know if someone is a psychopath or is at risk of becoming one?

Babiak, P., Neumann, C. S., and Hare, R. D. (2010). Corporate Psychopathy: Talking the Walk. *Behavioral Sciences & the Law*, *28*(2), 174–93.

Frick, P. J., Ray, J. V., Thornton, L. C., and Kahn, R. E. (2014). Annual Research Review: A Developmental Psychopathology Approach to Understanding Callous-Unemotional Traits in Children and Adolescents With Serious Conduct Problems. *Journal of Child Psychology and Psychiatry*, *55*(6), 532–48.

Hare, R. D., and Neumann, C. S. (2008). Psychopathy as a Clinical and Empirical Construct. *Annual Review of Clinical Psychology*, *4*, 217–46.

Pardini, D. A., Byrd, A. L., Hawes, S. W., and Docherty, M. (2018). Unique Dispositional Precursors to Early-Onset Conduct Problems and Criminal Offending in Adulthood. *Journal of the American Academy of Child & Adolescent Psychiatry*, *57*(8), 583–92.

Patrick, C. (ed.) (2018). *Handbook of Psychopathy* (2nd edn.). New York: The Guildford Press.

Chapter 2: Explaining the lack of empathy

Blair, R. J. R. (2013). The Neurobiology of Psychopathic Traits in Youths. *Nature Reviews Neuroscience*, *14*(11), 786–99.

Drayton, L. A., Santos, L. R., and Baskin-Sommers, A. (2018). Psychopaths Fail to Automatically Take the Perspective of Others. *Proceedings of the National Academy of Sciences*, *115*(13), 3302–7.

Schwenck, C., Mergenthaler, J., Keller, K., Zech, J., Salehi, S., Taurines, R., and Freitag, C. M. (2012). Empathy in Children with Autism and Conduct Disorder: Group-Specific Profiles and Developmental Aspects. *Journal of Child Psychology and Psychiatry*, *53*(6), 651–9.

Seara-Cardoso, A., and Viding, E. (2015). Functional Neuroscience of Psychopathic Personality in Adults. *Journal of Personality*, *83*(6), 723–37.

Chapter 3: Explaining impulsivity and failure to behave prosocially

Blair, R. J. R., Veroude, K., and Buitelaar, J. K. (2018). Neuro-Cognitive System Dysfunction and Symptom Sets: A Review of fMRI Studies in Youth with Conduct Problems. *Neuroscience & Biobehavioral Reviews*, *91*, 69–90.

Brazil, I. A., Mars, R. B., Bulten, B. H., Buitelaar, J. K., Verkes, R. J., and De Bruijn, E. R. (2011). A Neurophysiological Dissociation Between Monitoring One's Own and Others' Actions in Psychopathy. *Biological Psychiatry*, *69*(7), 693–9.

Foulkes, L., McCrory, E. J., Neumann, C. S., and Viding, E. (2014). Inverted Social Reward: Associations between Psychopathic Traits and Self-Report and Experimental Measures of Social Reward. *PLoS One*, *9*(8), e106000.

Hosking, J. G., Kastman, E. K., Dorfman, H. M., Samanez-Larkin, G. R., Baskin-Sommers, A., Kiehl, K. A., and Buckholtz, J. W. (2017). Disrupted Prefrontal Regulation of Striatal Subjective Value Signals in Psychopathy. *Neuron*, *95*(1), 221–31.

Sherman, E. D., and Lynam, D. R. (2017). Psychopathy and Low Communion: An Overlooked and Underappreciated Core Feature. *Personality Disorders: Theory, Research, and Treatment*, *8*(4), 309.

Viding, E., and McCrory, E. (2019). Towards Understanding Atypical Social Affiliation in Psychopathy. *Lancet Psychiatry*, *6*, 437–44.

Chapter 4: Why do some people become psychopaths?

Bedford, R., Pickles, A., Sharp, H., Wright, N., and Hill, J. (2015). Reduced Face Preference in Infancy: A Developmental Precursor to Callous-Unemotional Traits? *Biological Psychiatry*, *78*(2), 144–50.

Cecil, C. A., Lysenko, L. J., Jaffee, S. R., Pingault, J. B., Smith, R. G., Relton, C. L., and Barker, E. D. (2014). Environmental Risk, Oxytocin Receptor Gene (OXTR) Methylation and Youth Callous-Unemotional Traits: A 13-Year Longitudinal Study. *Molecular Psychiatry, 19*(10), 1071.

Dadds, M. R., Allen, J. L., Oliver, B. R., Faulkner, N., Legge, K., Moul, C., and Scott, S. (2012). Love, Eye Contact and the Developmental Origins of Empathy v. Psychopathy. *The British Journal of Psychiatry, 200*(3), 191–6.

Hyde, L. W., Waller, R., Trentacosta, C. J., Shaw, D. S., Neiderhiser, J. M., Ganiban, J. M., and Leve, L. D. (2016). Heritable and Nonheritable Pathways to Early Callous-Unemotional Behaviors. *American Journal of Psychiatry, 173*(9), 903–10.

Kimonis, E. R., Fanti, K. A., Isoma, Z., and Donoghue, K. (2013). Maltreatment Profiles Among Incarcerated Boys With Callous-Unemotional Traits. *Child Maltreatment, 18*(2), 108–21.

Viding, E., and McCrory, E. J. (2012). Genetic and Neurocognitive Contributions to the Development of Psychopathy. *Development and Psychopathology, 24*(3), 969–83.

Chapter 5: What to do with a psychopath?

Kiehl, K. A., and Hoffman, M. B. (2011). The Criminal Psychopath: History, Neuroscience, Treatment, and Economics. *Jurimetrics, 51*, 355.

Raine, A. (2018). The Neuromoral Theory of Antisocial, Violent, and Psychopathic Behavior. *Psychiatry Research*. Advance online publication.

Viding, E., and Jaffee, S. R. (2015). Genetic Issues and Antisocial Behaviour in Youth. *Science in the Courtroom, 1*(2).

Wilkinson, S., Waller, R., and Viding, E. (2016). Practitioner Review: Involving Young People With Callous Unemotional Traits in Treatment—Does it Work? A Systematic Review. *Journal of Child Psychology and Psychiatry, 57*(5), 552–65.

Further reading

Classic readings

Cleckley, H. (1941). *The Mask of Sanity*. St Louis, MO: Mosby.

Hare, R. D. (1999). *Without Conscience: The Disturbing World of the Psychopaths Among Us*. New York: The Guildford Press.

Edited volumes presenting research

DeLisi, M. (ed.). (2018). *Routledge International Handbook of Psychopathy and Crime*. London: Routledge.

Patrick, C. (ed.). (2018). *Handbook of Psychopathy* (2nd edn.). New York: The Guildford Press.

Salekin, R. T., and Lynam, D. R. (eds). (2010). *Handbook of Child and Adolescent Psychopathy*. New York: The Guildford Press.

Books on neurobiology of psychopathy

Blair, J., Mitchell, D., and Blair, K. (2005). *The Psychopath: Emotion and the Brain*. Malden: Blackwell Publishing.

Glenn, A. L., and Raine, A. (2014). *Psychopathy: An Introduction to Biological Findings and Their Implications*. New York: New York University Press.

Popular science books

Babiak, P., and Hare, R. D. (2007). *Snakes in Suits: When Psychopaths Go to Work*. New York: Harper Business.

Kiehl, K. A. (2015). *The Psychopath Whisperer: The Science of Those Without Conscience.* New York: Broadway Books.

Marsh, A. (2017). *The Fear Factor: How One Emotion Connects Altruists, Psychopaths, and Everyone In-Between.* New York: Basic Books.

Helpful websites

The Society for the Scientific Study of Psychopathy, https://www.psychopathysociety.org/en.

Aftermath: Surviving Psychopathy Foundation, https://aftermath-surviving-psychopathy.org.

Index

For the benefit of digital users, indexed terms that span two pages (e.g., 52–53) may, on occasion, appear on only one of those pages.

WITCHCRAFT
A Very Short Introduction
Malcolm Gaskill

Witchcraft is a subject that fascinates us all, and everyone knows
what a witch is - or do they? From childhood most of us develop a
sense of the mysterious, malign person, usually an old woman.
Historically, too, we recognize witch-hunting as a feature of pre-
modern societies. But why do witches still feature so heavily in our
cultures and consciousness? From Halloween to superstitions,
and literary references such as Faust and even Harry Potter,
witches still feature heavily in our society. In this Very Short
Introduction Malcolm Gaskill challenges all of this, and argues
that what we think we know is, in fact, wrong.

'Each chapter in this small but perfectly-formed book could be the
jumping-off point for a year's stimulating reading. Buy it now.'

Fortean Times

www.oup.com/vsi

SOCIAL MEDIA
Very Short Introduction

Join our community

www.oup.com/vsi

- Join us online at the official Very Short Introductions
  Facebook page.
- Access the thoughts and musings of our authors with our
  online **blog**.
- Sign up for our monthly **e-newsletter** to receive information
  on all new titles publishing that month.
- Browse the full range of Very Short Introductions online.
- Read **extracts** from the Introductions for free.
- Visit our library of **Reading Guides**. These guides, written by our
  expert authors will help you to question again, why you think
  what you think.
- If you are a teacher or lecturer you can order inspection
  copies quickly and simply via our website.

ONLINE CATALOGUE
A Very Short Introduction

Our online catalogue is designed to make it easy to find your ideal Very Short Introduction. View the entire collection by subject area, watch author videos, read sample chapters, and download reading guides.

http://fds.oup.com/www.oup.co.uk/general/vsi/index.html